SQUARE DANCING
everyone

Myrna Martin Schild

WITHDRAWN

DEDICATION

This book is dedicated to my mother and father, and others like them, who donated countless hours of selfless devotion toward the success and perpetuation of the progressive, new style of square dancing called the contemporary square dance movement. Special recognition is awarded to Bob Osgood who served as pioneer and leader for nearly half a century.

Inquiries should be addressed to the publisher:

 Hunter Textbooks Inc.

823 Reynolda Road
Winston-Salem, North Carolina 27104

FOREWORD

It will become obvious to you as you read through these pages that Professor Schild has a fond affection for square dancing. It's one thing to compile a collection of dance material and facts about square dancing; it's quite another to do it in such a manner that the author is obviously handing you a precious package. Square dancing and all that it encompasses is indeed that, an American heritage recognized by the Congress of the United States as the Folk Dance of America. With this text, you can do far more than learn and teach others to dance. You can share, by means of the well-written text and illustrations, a taste of their American heritage. Here is one subject so beautifully covered by Professor Schild, it will be of equal delight to both the students and the teachers. The beauty of this book is that one need not spend a lifetime in learning how to dance before passing this knowledge along to others. The use of this text will make the task a simple one and a course in American square dancing could very easily be one of the first to fill with students.

Bob Osgood

(Bob Osgood founded *Sets In Order American Square Dance Society* in 1948 and served as editor of *Square Dancing Magazine* until it ceased publication in December 1985. Among his numerous achievements are: Callerlab (the International Association of Square Dance Callers), Legacy, the Square Dance Hall of Fame, The Caller/Teacher Manual, The Caller/text, the Handbooks, etc.)

ABOUT THE AUTHOR

Myrna Martin Schild is Assistant Professor of Health, Physical Education and Recreation at Southern Illinois University at Edwardsville. She has been involved in square dance since the late 1940's and has witnessed many of its changes and dramatic expansion. She has served in the capacity of accomplished exhibitor, community club member, faculty advisor of contemporary square dance clubs and teacher of square dance at all levels of instruction in education. She has attended national and regional square dance conventions and has provided numerous demonstrations and exhibitions to further interest in square dancing.

Professor Schild has engaged in a variety of professional activities on the state, national and international levels of health, physical education and recreation. She is an active member of the National Dance Association and the International Relations Council (American Alliance of Health, Physical Education, Recreation and Dance) in which she has served on national committees and held national offices. She has taken trips around the world to research physical education and dance and has participated in World Congresses for the International Council of Health, Physical Education and Recreation which is under the auspices of UNESCO (United Nations Educational, Scientific and Cultural Organization) with members in well over 200 countries. She has found the presence of American square dance in most of the countries she has visited around the world (Europe, Africa, the Mideast, the Orient, the Pacific, Central and South America). It is truly an international language.

Professor Schild is also the author of the textbook *Social Dance* and its accompanying one and one-half hour instructional videotape. Both are available from the author. Please address inquiries to Myrna Martin Schild, Box 1126 — Dance, Southern Illinois University at Edwardsville, Edwardsville, Illinois, 62026-1126.

PREFACE

Square dancing is considered to be the American form of folk dance. Its popularity has endured for almost 300 years and has grown measurably in modern times. Several million people view square dance as an international language of friendship and continue to attend regularly square dances all over the world. This book explains the development, the basic movements and suggested dance drills of both traditional and contemporary square dance.

The primary objectives of this book are to provide the novice dancer with a simplified analysis of the basic techniques of square dance, to show the fun and challenge of square dance and to instill an interest in square dance which could carry over into community level dancing as a lifetime activity.

The material in this text is organized so that the beginner will gradually be introduced to the basics of square dance. Learning quantities of new movements quickly does not comply with the author's intentions. The basics should be learned, one by one, and then applied to an actual dance. This should help the dancer to feel more confident and allow a feeling of instant success. The teacher or caller will continue to "stack the calls" in a manner which is contingent upon the average learning rate of the class as whole. During each session, the students should be stimulated mentally, physically and socially. Square dancing is a very healthful activity. It develops excellent recall or memory. It reduces stress and relieves tension by encouragement of ability to relax and have fun. It also is an excellent source of physical exercise and has been recommended by many physicians as a regular activity. The social aspect of each session should be stressed so that the students will become acquainted with each other and make the class experience even more meaningful.

The basic movements of square dancing are standardized so as to allow worldwide participation. This book is consistent with the most recent information available. As a supplement to this text, the square dance enthusiast should have access to the most recent edition of the handbook entitled *The Illustrated Basic and Mainstream Movements of Square Dancing* (price approximately $1.00), and square dancer's bible, *The Caller/Teacher Manual* (price approximately $30.00). These sources are invaluable aids and have served as the primary instruments of research for this book. The national square dance magazine is entitled *American Square Dance* and is published monthly in Huron, Ohio. (Another national square dance magazine entitled *Square Dancing* was published by *Sets In Order American Square Dance Society* from 1948 until 1985.)

Contact the author if you are interested in an instructional videotape to accompany this book. Visual lessons provide a real advantage in the learning process. Availability will be subject to demand.

ACKNOWLEDGMENTS

I wish to extend appreciation to those who helped in the preparation of this book. The half-tones were prepared by my husband, Jim, who is also an author and a photographer. Posing for his photos was the Southern Illinois University at Edwardsville Square Dance Club, the *Cougar Squares*. Club President, Glen Martin, provided numerous sources of information. He and Dr. Zadia Herrold, Chairman of Health, Recreation and Physical Education at Southern Illinois University at Edwardsville for twenty years, encouraged me to write this book. Bob Osgood, founder of *Sets In Order American Square Dance Society* and editor of *Square Dancing Magazine* from 1948-1985, permitted me to use his line drawings as illustrative material for this book. He also provided back copies of his magazine for research purposes and offered his expertise and guidance. Other consultants for specific areas of the book were: traditional square dance — Dr. Bill Litchman, curator of the Lloyd "Pappy" Shaw Foundation Archives Center; Big Circle mountain dancing and clogging — Professor Don Allen, physical education teacher and square dance caller at the University of Northern Iowa; in St. Louis, Missouri: contemporary square dance — Bo Semith, physical education teacher and professional square dance caller; clubs — Richard E. Riggs; John Higgens, fiddle teacher who provided old-time fiddle tunes; and Roy and Dorothy Gleason, record experts from Webster Record Shop.

Contents

Part One — Getting Started

General information is necessary in order to acquaint the novice with the history, requirements, positions and procedures of all square dance

Chapter one

Background and Development

Square dance was a significant part of America's growth. It originated in New England with the early colonists and later spread westward with the pioneers and their ox-driven Conestoga. At first, because of the Puritan influence, dancing was condemned and its primary instrument, the fiddle, was regarded as the "voicebox of Lucifer." But, like so many devices of the Devil, the activity could not be suppressed.

This is illustrated by one of the stories about the legendary Davy Crockett. One day, as he was walking through the woods, he heard the tantalizing sawstroke of a fiddle-tune. He was beckoned by the sound and came to a flooded creek. Stranded in the middle of the high water was a fiddle-playing preacher in a stalled buggy. Davy demanded to know why the preacher-man was "a-roostin' in the middle of a flood a-worshippin' the Devil?" The clergyman contended that he could have yelled "'til ole Satan himself come fer him and nary a soul would help, but if'n he'd play the fiddle and there was a sinner within 20 mile, he'd come a-runnin', and durned if'n he didn't."

Rural families had to be self-sufficient, providing their own food, clothing and entertainment. It was rare to find a family unit that did not have its own fiddler or banjo player. Each generation was responsible for teaching the next generation to play music and to dance. Square dancing was the primary form of social recreation. It was common for whole communities to congregate for a barn-raising, a quilting bee, a corn huskin', molasses makin' or other activities. Whether its location was in a New England Town Hall, a Grange Hall of the Plains or a western barn, after the work was completed it was time for some fun and the square dance would begin. Young people thought nothing of walking for miles through adverse conditions to get to an evening of square dancing. They would refuse to sit down between dances because they would lose their coveted places at "top o' the set" (head couples).

Early figures were simple and repetitious. They could be learned and enjoyed in one evening. The format of each dance usually consisted of an introductory call, a basic figure in which all four couples took turns performing the same basic calls, a break in the middle, and a conclusion at the end. This basic format was developed from a variety of regional influences.

The New England dancers were trained on English reels, court quadrilles, country dances and contras in lines. Set patterns were followed through the aid of a prompter or caller. "The Virginia Reel" was a very popular dance from the East. The Appalachian Mountains were known for having adopted the English running set which consists of a large circle of couples who dance to a caller who "chooses the changes to his fancy." (This developed into modern style hash calling.) The mountain areas also adopted fast-fiddlin' sounds and clogging or flat-footin' dance steps. "Sourwood Mountain" is an example of the southern Appalachian fiddle-style. Other old time hoedown tunes played in duple rhythm are "Boil (Bile) the Cabbage Down," "Old Joe Clark," "Sally Goodin'," "Soldier's Joy," "The Arkansas Traveller" and many more. Some dances became identified with popular old-time songs, such as "Darling Nellie Gray" and "Red River Valley."

After the westward expansion, Texas developed a flowery, ornamental slower style so as to allow the two-step dance patterns. The square dance known as "The Texas Star" was an all-time favorite. In California, a slow, smooth style that required a graceful, gliding walk eventually evolved and became the footwork style used by modern square dancers today.

French quadrilles, Irish jigs, Spanish fandangos and German mazurkas have also influenced the development of American

Figure 1-1. Square dancing is a strong part of American heritage and culture. (Photo courtesy of *New England Square Dancer Caller Magazine,* Lowell, Massachusetts.)

square dancing. The "Do-sa-do" was derived from the French item, "dos a' dos," which means back-to-back. The "Allemande" was probably developed from a German folk dance of the same name.

In the 1920's, Mr. and Mrs. Henry Ford contributed greatly to square dance research. Otherwise, little was changed in square dancing until the World War II era. In 1939, Dr. Lloyd "Pappy" Shaw wrote a book entitled *Cowboy Dances* in which he stressed his philosophy of the significance of square dancing in America. He strongly believed in the preservation of American heritage and that square dance was an important part of it. He organized many classes to teach America's recreational leaders about this American folk art which is considered to be the national dance. The background of square dancing makes it as American as the Declaration of Independence or the Fourth of July. "Pappy" Shaw's followers became the system through which the information was relayed to the communities around the nation.

After World War II, interest in square dance grew quickly as a national recreational pastime. One reason was that returning servicemen were reunited with their women and wanted to laugh, socialize and have fun. The expansion of square dancing refers not only to the number of people involved but also to the amount of time they devoted to the activity. It went from a once a month to a weekly affair. During the mid-forties and early fifties, active dancers desired more than the simple, repetitive figures of the traditional dances. The visiting couple patterns progressed into the activation of two couples moving simultaneously around the two inactive couples. This grid-work initiated more movement. Innumerable new formations were developed and this resulted in the creation of new basics.

It was only natural that the callers would try different combinations of these basics so that their pattern calls would be more interesting and more challenging. This became known as "hashing the calls" or "hash." Its popularity was equal to that of the singing calls — which also underwent some changes in the process of becoming modernized. The

Figure 1-2. Square dancing conventions have been held in the United States since the 1950's. (Photo courtesy of *New England Square Dance Caller Magazine,* Lowell, Massachusetts.)

dancers wanted to dance to contemporary music and lyrics. It was discovered that almost any popular song could be converted to a square dance. This emphasized the use of different instruments and more choreography. The improved quality of public address systems made it feasible for callers to communicate with large groups of dancers. Also, these dancers had more time for recreation due to shorter working hours and they found it easier to travel to the dances because of better automobiles and road conditions. Many people who found the footwork in social dancing especially difficult actually preferred square dancing and most local communities accommodated them by forming square dance clubs. Printed literature on the new type of square dancing helped to organize the movement and it quickly spread to the state, national and international levels.

Since the 1950's those organizations have blossomed into what is currently an actual support system:

1. Square dance publications which consist of locally circulated newsletters and national magazines. In 1948, The *Sets in Order American Square Dance Society (SIO-ASDS)* was formed. This society published *Square Dancing Magazine*, which became the voice of square dancing everywhere. Its headquarters are located in Los Angeles where it houses the Square Dance Hall of Fame and maintains an archives and communications center on the historical background of square dancing. It also provides a scholarship program for the proper training of prospective callers. *SIO-ASDS*, under the direction of Bob Osgood, developed most of the support system.

2. *Callerlab* is the *International Association of Square Dance Callers*. It is officially responsible for accrediting square dance callers and for other concerns about callers and basics.

3. The Annual National Square Dance Convention began in the early fifties and has attracted tens of thousands of dancers each year during early summer.

4. The Lloyd Shaw Foundation helps to regulate contemporary square dance forms by reminding square dancers of their traditional past.

5. *Legacy* is the overall communications group for all of the square dance support sytem.

6. The *Overseas Dancers Association* and *C.R.O.W.D.* provide information for square dancers who relocate or travel away from home and wish to find or communicate with dancers in another geographical area.

7. Square Dance Week occurs annually during the third full week of September and is coordinated and promoted on a worldwide basis.

8. *Bachelors 'n' Bachelorettes, Inc.* has chapters in many cities for single square dancers.

It is evident that square dancing has become a highly organized activity. In the late fifties, a list of 20 basic calls was devised by *Sets In Order*. In the early sixties, this list was expanded to include 10 more basics for the high frequency dancers. In 1969, the *Sets In Order American Square Dance Society* published a booklet entitled "The Basic Movements of Square Dancing — Basic 50," designed for what it designated as the first plateau level. Later, *SIO-ASDS* printed another booklet entitled "The Extended Basic Movements of Square Dancing (51-75)" in addition to the first plateau level and designated it as the second plateau. The third plateau was strictly for experimental and challenge or advanced high-level dancing. In 1974, 10 more basics were added to bring the total to 85 extended basics which were later selected to be the Mainstream Movements of contemporary square dancing.

At the Callerlab Convention of 1981, a list of Basic Movements and Mainstream Movements was standardized. This process was instigated because of the rapid growth and development of square dance in modern times. New calls are created monthly and are taught to high-level, challenge dancers in workshops. Some of these calls will be selected quarterly to be added to the Mainstream and Mainstream Plus lists. Presumably, under the auspices of the Callerlab system, a square dancer will be able to attend a square dance anywhere and be confident of dancing to standardized calls and basic movements.

Chapter two

The Novice Dancer

Welcome to the delightful domain of square dancing! You will be learning a language that probably is new to you, but some of these terms have been used in traditional square dancing for more than 250 years. Only the movements which have been time-tested through continuous usage become the accepted basics of square dance. They must be necessary movements that are short, clear, smooth-flowing and easy to learn. All of the basic movements described in this book meet these requirements.

It has been said that it takes eighty-six times of practicing a basic before a dancer will perform it automatically when called upon to do so. Repetition is of great importance in the learning process. People learn at different rates of speed. Some dancers adjust quickly and others need to be coaxed and encouraged.

Do not become impatient with yourself or with others in your class if learning speed becomes a problem. Novice dancers often need extra support during the initial period of adjustment. The teacher or caller can help the situation by obtaining a record player with variable speed control so that the dancers do not have to feel rushed.

The four requirements of a proper square dance session are:

1. Four couples, preferably male-female combination, in each set;

2. A spacious facility with a smooth floor (in olden days, the wide boards had more spring and were more fun);

3. Lively music which usually consists of special square dance records;

4. A teacher or caller.

Forming Squares and Positions

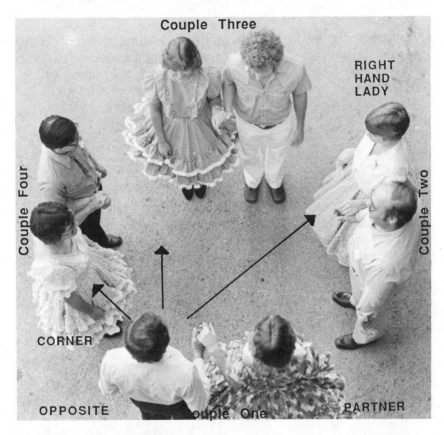

Figure 2-1. The couples above are in the square position to start a dance.

All four couples face in to the center of the square with the back of each couple parallel to a different wall of the hall. The designated "home" positions for Couples One through Four are counterclockwise from Couple One who is stationed with backs toward the front of the hall. Couple Two is to the right of Couple One. Couple Three is opposite Couple One and these two couples are collectively called Head couples. Couple Four is opposite Couple Two and these two couples are collectively called Side couples. The man's partner is on his right and the next lady (to his right) is designated the right hand lady. The lady directly across the set is his opposite. The lady on the man's left is his corner. Opposite couples should maintain a distance of 7-10 feet, the lesser amount being preferred because it keeps the square more compact.

Posture

Dancers should be aware of good postural habits. They should stand erect with head up, shoulders square and slightly back, chest lifted, abdomen and gluteals tight and weight centered over both feet. Posture should be dynamic so as to be ready for the next movement. Arms also should be slightly flexed.

Hand Positions

It is essential to distinguish the right hand from the left hand in square dancing. Most calls involve different uses of the hands and the caller choreographs the patterns with appropriate hand changes. The dancer should be ready to extend the free hand for the next call, but should never anticipate (or move prior to the directions of) the caller.

Couple Handhold

The couple has inside hands joined as they stand side by side facing the same direction. The man's palm is up and the lady's palm is down. The arms are bent and the hands are slightly above elbow height. While awaiting the next call in the square, the man should hold the lady's hand. In couple position, the man is on the left.

Figure 2-2. Author Myrna Schild and her husband, Jim Schild, demonstrate the proper couple handhold.

Forearm Hold

Facing dancers place the hand on the inside of the arm of the other person so that the hand is between their wrist and elbow joint.

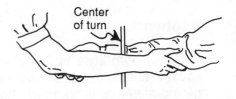

Figure 2-3. Forearm hold.

Handshake Hold

The dancers shake hands at about waist height with the thumb overlapping the back of the other dancer's hand.

Figure 2-4. Handshake hold.

Loose Handhold

The dancers allow enough pressure so as to revolve hands around each other while continuing to maintain physical contact.

Figure 2-5. Loose handhold.

Hands Up Hold

Facing dancers use a crossed-palm position. The palms are touching with fingers pointing up and the hand then tilts slightly outward.

Figure 2-6. Hands up hold.

Footwork

The western style of footwork has been adopted by modern square dancing. It should emphasize a smooth, effortless gliding step that is taken on the ball of the foot before the heel is lowered gently to the floor. The old-time foot stomping, hopping and jumping are taboo and inappropriate in the modern style of dancing. The stride should be short and most of the movement is from the knees down to the feet. The name of this modern style of footwork is the shuffle step.

Timing

Most basic movements require 4 counts of music. For example, it takes 4 steps to walk across the set, make a hand turn, make a courtesy turn or to perform a basic swing. It takes 16 counts to circle full around for 8 dancers to return to home position. It requires 8 counts to complete a do sa do, grand right and left or right and left thru. On a metronome, square dance music has about 128-150 beats per minute. The caller has to be very conscious of timing so that the dancers can coordinate their movements and move in unison. The dancers should always move after the caller gives the directions. Never anticipate the calls. Always move to the beat of the music and emphasize smooth body flow. The caller usually directs his calls to the man.

Dress

A western type of attire has been adopted by square dancers. The woman wears a blouse or dress with ruffles and a full skirt. A petticoat made of yards of stiff material is worn under the skirt. Her shoes are relatively flat with leather soles. The man wears a western shirt or vest, western belt, tie, pants and boots or boot-shoes. Square dancers enjoy wearing this type of clothing and it serves the purposes of allowing freedom of movement and identifying dancers as square dancers.

Skirtwork

The lady holds her skirt about waist level with the hand that is free and she waves it from front to back as she performs certain movements. Callerlab specifies which movements require skirtwork.

Structure

A typical contemporary square dance consists of a series of tips or components of which each includes a singing call dance, a hash call dance and a respite or rest which allows time for Round Dancing (which is a type of social dancing that is danced in a large circle and precisely timed and choreographed to contemporary music).

Singing Calls. As the name implies, singing calls have a definite melody and the directions are sung by the caller. One pattern usually is repeated for the introduction, break (or middle) and conclusion. Another part of the dance called the figure usually is repeated 4 times so that the dancers continue to change partners until the men get their original partners back home. Singing calls usually are choreographed to contemporary music.

Hash. As the name implies, hash calls are a mixture of basic movements, chosen and choreographed by the caller. The caller has the responsibility, after a series of various calls used for the purpose of position changes, to return the dancers to their home positions. They usually finish the pattern with an allemande left to the original corner and follow up with a partner promenade shortly thereafter. The music selected by the caller should be a type of hoedown played in duple or cut-time. Since it is not possible to memorize the sequences in hash calling, the dancers must listen carefully so as to follow the directions given by the caller. This type of square dancing presents a real challenge to the dancers and they usually show their excitement if they can finish the pattern. They know they have made it when they hear the call "Allemande left." The dancers must know the calls extremely well before attempting actual hash dancing at a square dance.

Laws and Courtesies

1. Square up quickly. If more couples are needed to complete the square, raise one hand and indicate the number of couples needed by lifting the same number of fingers.

2. Be a good listener. Do not clap hands or stomp feet while dancing.

3. Be courteous and friendly. At the end of the tip, thank others.

4. Be clean and well-dressed. Square dance is a close-contact activity and good grooming habits are essential.

5. Be patient with others and yourself if mistakes are made.

6. Be sociable, mingling with other dancers. Do not form cliques.

7. Have fun and try to see that others also have fun.

Message to Novice Dancers

Initially, it is imperative to learn to react to the calls and to the seven other dancers in your square. Know which direction and who to face before and after each call. Solid foundations will last throughout your square dancing lifetime.

Chapter three

Rudiments
of Traditional and
Contemporary Square Dance

It is essential to learn some introductory basics before proceeding. These are the fundamentals of all square dance and are used in both the traditional and the contemporary styles.

Circle Family

In a Circle, two or more dancers join hands and move forward to the left, unless the direction is specified to the right.

Forward and Back

Each individual dancer walks forward three steps to pause on count four without transferring weight and lightly touches the foot to the floor to keep time. The dancer then reverses direction using the opposite foot to repeat the sequence. When meeting the opposite person, outside palms may touch in acknowledgment.

Do Sa Do

Similar to Dos a Dos, Do Sa, Do Si, Sashay, All 'Round the Left Hand Lady, with the Do Sa Do, two facing dancers advance to pass right shoulders (right shoulder is forward), move to the right (without turning), move back-to-back and continue to complete the circle by passing left shoulders (left shoulder is forward and moving backward to place). The accepted hand position for men is at the waist with the elbows bent outward. The woman uses skirtwork.

See Saw. A See Saw is the opposite movement of a Do Sa Do. It starts by passing left shoulders. It often follows a Do Sa Do and this sequence forms a figure eight.

Swing

The Swing is often accompanied by a Bow in traditional square dancing. In a Bow, the men bend forward at the waist and the ladies curtsy. The Swing consists of a couple moving together and revolving around a central pivot point for four or more counts.

Waist Swing. In the Waist Swing, the couple face each other with right sides together and assume a modified social dance position in which the man's left hand holds the lady's right hand about shoulder high. He places his right palm on her back above her left waist. She places her left hand on his right upper arm near the shoulder. Posture should be erect, but the dancers can lean back slightly from the waist up.

Figure 3-1. Waist swing.

Footwork. The footwork can begin with the walk-around step (which is performed as the name implies) and lead gradually to the "buzz step" in which the left foot pushes on the outside of the turning circle and the right foot moves up and down in place. The footwork is identical for the man and the lady. Their right feet are secured against each other to eliminate hopping or jerking. It is very smooth and rhythmic and is performed in unison with the partner. It is similar to riding a child's scooter (in a tight circle) where the right foot "scoots" and the left foot pushes. The feet should be kept in short-step position. Practice leading into and breaking out of the Swing smoothly. It can end with a twirl which is an underarm turn in which the man raises his left arm and the lady's right arm so that the lady can make a full clockwise turn.

Figure 3-2. Footwork for the swing step.

Drill

(Formations can be square or a large circle of couples.)

These basics can be combined into a sequence and could be called to square dance music. This is a suggested combination:

All join hands and circle to the left
Back to the right and square your set
Do Sa Do the corner
See Saw the partner
Everybody go Forward up and Back (toward the center and
   "holler")
Swing your own

(Note: If a circular formation is used with a large group, this drill can lead into the next basic, a promenade, using an old favorite, the Grand March. Refer to Appendix A for directions.)

Promenade Family

A Promenade is simply walking in a counterclockwise direction (unless otherwise specified). Promenades are full, 1/2, 3/4.

Couples. When couples Promenade, the man is on the inside and the lady is on the outside in couple position.

The hands and arms are in skater's position with right hands joined on top and left hands joined on bottom. The man's palm can face up while the lady's palm faces down or reverse. They Promenade until arriving at the man's home position unless otherwise directed.

Figure 3-3. Promenade handhold.

Single File. In a Single File Promenade, the dancers move one in front of the other in a counterclockwise direction or to the right. One or even all four of the women (or men) may be asked to Promenade on the inside or on the outside of the square. The ladies work their skirts.

Wrong Way. In a Wrong Way Promenade, the dancers reverse direction (clockwise).

Refer to Appendix A for a simple, old-time Singing Call involving a Circle, Swing and Promenade ("Marching Thru Georgia," Windsor #4112).

Allemande Family (Arm Swings)

An Allemande consists of two facing dancers who use the proper arm to walk around each other, drop hands and return to face the next person designated by the caller. A forearm grip should be used so as to shorten the radius of the turn. The man cups his hand under the lady's arm with his thumb held in and the lady simply rests her hand firmly on the man's forearm, not past the elbow joint. The center of the turn will be near the middle of the joined arms so that the dancers are equidistant from each other as they move.

Allemande Left. Face the corner for an Allemande using left forearms to end facing the partner.

Allemande Right. Face the designated dancer for an Allemande using right forearms and turn to face the corner.

Left Arm Turn. Using left forearms, turn the specified distance (1/2, 3/4, full).

Right Arm Turn. Using right forearms, turn the specified distance (1/2, 3/4, full).

Refer to Appendix A for a simple, old-time Singing Call ("Oh, Johnny, Oh," Blue Star #1690).

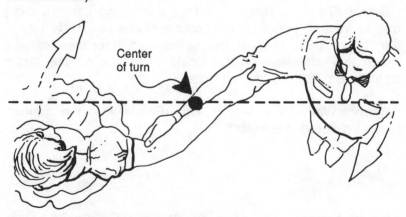

Center of turn

Figure 3-4. Allemande turn.

Right and Left Grand Family

In a Right and Left Grand, partners face (at home position usually) and join their right hands. They pull by, moving forward (the man travels in a counterclockwise direction and the lady travels clockwise) to extend an alternate hand, about waist high, to each person of the opposite sex coming toward them. Each hand should be released as the dancers pass each other and then the free hand should be extended to the next person. When the partner is retrieved, the dancers should await the next call. The Right and Left Grand often follows an Allemande Left, but these are separate calls and should not be joined automatically.

Weave the Ring. The Weave the Ring is similar to a Right and Left Grand except hands do not touch. The hand and arm positions are the same as in the Do Sa Do.

Wrong Way Grand. A Wrong Way Grand is the same as a Right and Left Grand except the traveling directions are reversed.

Drill

A simple combination of these calls would be:

Allemande Left with your left hand
Partner right go Right and Left Grand
Every other girl with every other hand
Meet your partner and Promenade home

Star Family

In a star formation, the designated dancers move to the center to make contact with a palm star hand position in which the fingers are pointing upward and the palms are touching. The Star is turned by walking forward the designated distance (1/4, 1/2, 3/4 or once around). The ladies use skirtwork with the outside hand.

Star by the Right. The Star is formed by using the right hand.

Star by the Left. The Star is formed by using the left hand.

Star Promenade. Using a modified couple position, a Star is formed by specified dancers using the designated hand. The partners are travelling in the same direction and place the arm that is toward each other around each other's waist. The Star Promenade advances a specified distance.

Figure 3-5. Star Promenade.

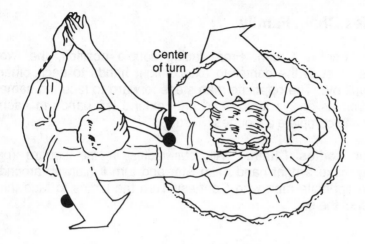

Figure 3-6. Courtesy Turn.

Courtesy Turn

The Courtesy Turn can start from couple position or from a position where two dancers are facing. The purpose is to reverse direction while maintaining a modified couple position. The lady gives the man her left palm (down) to his left palm (up). He places his right hand in the small of her back while she places her right hand on her right waist or on her skirt for skirtwork. The couple makes a counterclockwise turn as the man backs up and the lady moves forward. They usually end the move by facing the center of the set.

Ladies Chain Family

Two Ladies Chain. From facing couple position, the two ladies meet in the center to extend right hands to each other and pull by. The opposite man steps forward to face the same direction as she is facing and they extend left hands to each other and complete a Courtesy Turn.

Four Ladies Chain. All four ladies in the square (or circle) make a right hand palm Star and turn it halfway around to the opposite men who Courtesy Turn the ladies to face the center of the set.

Ladies Chain Three Quarters—Two/Four Ladies Chain

This figure is similar to the other Ladies Chains except it requires travelling 3/4 instead of 1/2 the distance around the set.

Refer to Appendix A for a simple, old-time Singing Call involving a Ladies Chain ("Comin' Round the Mountain," Windsor #4115).

Part Two — Traditional Square Dancing

Introduction

Traditional square dancing should not be regarded as a beautiful antique, but as a living folk art. These dances have weathered the test of time and continue to bring pleasure to their participants. Some figures had their origins in Europe and many can be traced to the historical beginnings of America. Clubs still exist that specialize in performing and exhibiting the traditional dances so as to preserve their beauty and cultural value as an art form.

Chapter four

Visiting Couple Figures

The visiting couple figure is elementary to many traditional square dances. Usually, Couple One leads to the right to Couple Two and a specific pattern is performed. When completed, Couple One continues the cycle by visiting Couple Three and finally Couple Four. The same pattern is performed with each couple until Couple One returns to their home position.

Birdie in the Cage (Cage the Bird)

Call: The first top couple lead to the right and circle four
Birdie in the Cage, and shut the door
Birdie hops out and the crow flies in
Crow flies out and gives her a spin

The designated couple leads to the right to join hands and Circle left with the next couple. The lead lady (the bird) steps into the center of the circle to "chirp" and hop, imitating a bird. Next, the caller tells the bird to hop out and crow (the lead man) to fly in. They exchange places. The man flaps his wings and "caws" like a crow. Then the man returns to the outside circle to Swing his partner. This figure is repeated with each consecutive couple.

A variation is to add each couple gradually to the outside circle as they finish each part. After the lead couple completes the pattern with the last couple, all four couples Circle to the left to their home positions.

Duck for the Oysters (Dig for the Clams)

Call: The first couple lead to the right and Circle half
You Duck for the Oysters
You Dig for the Clams
You duck for the way to the happy land

This dance is performed to the tune of "Hinkey Dinkey, Parlez Vous." To Duck for the Oysters, the designated couple leads to the right to join hands and Circle left half-way around. The two couples have exchanged places. Keeping hands joined, the inside couple makes an arch first and the lead couple ducks under it as far as they can go and returns to place on the outside of the set. To "Dig for the Clams," the lead couple makes an arch and the other couple ducks under as before.

The figure ends with the inside couple again making an arch so that the lead couple can duck through (releasing hands with the other couple) and repeat the figure with the next couple in the set. When every couple has finished the pattern, they also take turns leading the entire sequence.

Figure 4-1. Duck for the Oysters, (Dig for the Clams).

Figure 8 (Grapevine Twist)

Call: Top couple to the right and gent lead 'round
Make your Figure 8 so sound
Around the lady, around the gent
Now hurry for your time is spent

The designated gent takes his partner by the inside hand and leads to the right to the next couple. He continues to lead his partner around the lady of that couple, makes a Figure 8 in the center and returns to travel between that couple to move around the gent. The two couples then join hands in a circle, and the lead couple moves on to the next couple in the set. A variation is for the lead gent to drop the hand of the other couple lady (in the circle) and repeat the figure by leading all three dancers around the lady of the next consecutive couple. Gradually, Couple Three and finally Couple Four are added to the line. (This can become "crack the whip" — the last person in line hangs on tight.) Then all four couples Circle until the home position is reached. Each couple in the set takes their turn to lead the figure.

Hot Time in the Old Town

Singing Call: There'll be a hot time in the old town tonight
The first couple out and Circle four hands 'round
And you pick up two and Circle six hands 'round
And you pick up two and Circle eight hands 'round
There'll be a hot time in the old town tonight

Chorus: Allemande Left with the lady on the left
Allemande Right with the lady on the right
Allemande Left with the lady on the left
And Grand old Right and Left around the ring

The designated couple leads to the couple on the right, and they join hands and Circle to the left all the way around. The lead man breaks the circle (keeping his partner on his right) and picks up each consecutive couple (keeping them in order) after circling once around. The chorus starts with an Allemande Left to the corner, pass the partner and Allemande

Right the lady on the right (right hand lady), pass the partner again to Allemande Left the corner once more and Grand Right and Left. Meet the partner and Promenade home. Repeat with each couple taking turns as the lead couple.

Inside Arch, Outside Under (Dip 'n' Dive)

Call: First couple lead to the right
        Circle half and don't you blunder
        Inside Arch and Outside Under
        Dip 'n' Dive and away you go
        The inside high, the outside low
        Dip 'n' Dive across the track
        Dip 'n' Dive a-comin' back
        When you all get straight
        Promenade home and Swing all eight

The specified couple leads to the right to Circle half so that the lead couple is on the outside of the set. Drop hands with the

Figure 4-2. Inside Arch, Outside Under (Dip 'n' Dive).

other couple. The first side couple (on the inside) makes an arch, and the lead couple (on the outside) dives under to make an arch for the second side couple (straight across the set) to dive under. Any time a couple is facing out, they need to turn 1/2 to face in. (A California Twirl, found in Part Three of this text, would be an appropriate move.) The couples continue to "dip 'n' dive" until the side couples are home again, and the lead couple is in the center to Swing to their home position. If the caller wants to extend this figure, he can have the lead couple (instead of swinging home, visit the second head couple (across the set) to perform a call or two to acknowledge them. The lead couple leaves them and visits the second side couple to Circle half and repeat the "Dip 'n' Dive" figure again until everyone can Swing at home.

Pop Goes the Weasel

Singing Call: The first top lady leads to the right
        And don't you dare to blunder
        Circle three hands 'round you go
        Pop the lady under
        The lady and gent lead to the right
        And Circle three hands 'round you
        That's the way the monkey goes
        Pop goes the Weasel

Figure 4-3. Pop Goes the Weasel.

In this dance, the weasel is the lady, and she is chased by the monkey who is the gent. The designated couple lady leads to the couple on the right, and all three Circle to the left. On the command to "pop" the lady (or the weasel), the lead lady goes through the arch made by the other two, and she joins the next couple to the right. This time, the lead gent completes the figure with the couple on his right (the same couple the lady has now left). Both the lead lady and the lead gent that follows her are "popped" under on command. They Swing in the center of the set and can either Swing home (to end the figure) or continue to visit each couple in the set with the basic pattern. Each couple takes their turn as the lead couple.

Take a Peek

Call: First couple Bow and Swing
Lead on out to the right of the ring
Go around that couple, and take a peek
Back to your own, and swing your sweet (or cheat)
Around that couple, and peek once more
Circle up four in the middle of the floor

Figure 4-4. Take a Peek.

The directed couple leads to the couple on the right where the lead couple continues to hold inside hands and leans forward to "peek" at each other behind the first side couple. Then the lead couple Swings (or the lady may "cheat" by swinging the inactive gent of the first side couple). Repeat the "peeking" figure with the Swing. The two couples then Circle (to the left). The pattern is repeated with each consecutive couple until the lead couple can Swing to their home position. Each couple takes turns as the lead couple.

Figure 4-5. All ages, from tots to seniors, can perform and enjoy traditional square dancing.

Chapter five

Other Popular Traditional Dances

Chase the Rabbit

Call: Chase the rabbit; chase the squirrel
Chase that pretty girl 'round the world
Now chase that possum; chase that 'coon
Chase that big boy around the room

The intended lady leads to the right, and her partner follows. They travel single file around the outside of the square until the caller indicates that they reverse directions (Chase the possum). They return home and Swing. As a variation, this figure also could be performed facing another couple for a Figure Eight call starting with the lady leading around the lady and the gent following.

Lone Gents (Right Hand Over, Left Hand Under)

Call: The first top couple lead to the right and Circle four
Leave your lady where she be, Gent pass on to Circle three
Take a lady with you once more; Lead to the last and Circle four
Leave that lady on her own; Top gent goes home alone

Chorus: Forward six and a-back you go; Two lone gents do a Do Sa Do
Right hand lady high, left hand lady low

33

Figure 5-1. Lone Gents (Right Hand Over, Left Hand Under); Head couple is ready to circle with Couple Four to complete the figure.

This dance is an expanded version of a visiting couple pattern. The designated couple leads to the couple on the right to circle to the left once around. The lead gent leaves his partner with the first side couple so that the first side gent is standing in a line of three between his own partner who is on his right and the lead gent's partner standing on his left. The lead gent has progressed to the second head couple to Circle left once around. He takes this lady's left hand in his right hand and leads her to the second side couple (leaving the second head gent to stand alone) where they circle three to the left once around. He then leaves that lady with the second side couple in a line of three (as before) and he goes home alone. In the chorus, the two lines of three go forward and back (four counts each) and the two lone gents do a Do Sa Do. On the next call, the side gents make an arch by lifting the right arm to allow the head couple ladies to duck under the arch and move to the lone gent on his nearest side to her. Simultaneously, the side couple ladies, after making an arch, also move to the nearest side of the lone gent. He now is standing between two ladies and the other two gents have become the lone gents. The chorus is repeated until the original partner is on each gent's right side and the original corner is on the gent's left side.

Rip 'n' Snort

Call: First ole couple Rip 'n' Snort
Go down the middle and cut 'em off short
The lady go "Gee"; The gent go "Haw"
Get back home to your mother-in-law

While all eight Circle to the left, the lead couple dives through an arch made by the opposite couple. The active couple releases each other's hands so that the man can lead his line to the left and the lady can lead her line to the right. Everyone else keeps hands joined. The couple that made the arch turns outward under their own arms to face into the center. A circle is formed again and the figure is repeated with the next consecutive couple leading. A variation is to keep all hands joined throughout so that the lead couple has to pull everyone through an arch they have made also by turning under their own arms. Any couple can Rip 'n' Snort; the prettiest couple, the smartest couple, the best couple and the shortest couple are examples.

Figure 5-2. Rip 'n' Snort.

Texas Star

Call: Ladies to the center and back to the bar
Gent go in for a Right Hand Star
Right hand across, "How do ya do?"
Left hand back and "How are you?"
Meet your pretty girl; pass her by
Catch the next girl on the fly
Gents back out; the ladies go in
Make that Texas Star again
Ladies back out; the gent go in
One more star and you're gone again
Gents back out and everybody swing

The four ladies go forward to the center and backward to home position. (The partners can join right hands while the ladies go to the center back-to-back and then return to their home positions via a left-face counterclockwise underarm turn.) All four gents make a Right Hand Star, then change to a Left Hand Star, pass their partners to take the right hand lady for a Star Promenade. The gents back out (ladies remain in Star Promenade position), turn 1/2 or 1 1/2 times so that the ladies can go in for a reverse Star Promenade. The gents back out and everybody Swings. Repeat until the original partners are reunited.

Clogging

Mountain clogging is an individual type of dance that is traditionally performed to hoedown music. The torso is almost stationary (except for some arm motion) while the footwork consists of intricate movements. Clogging originated in the fancy steps of the Irish and English settlers of the mountainous areas — Appalachians, Smokies, Ozarks, etc. It is also called "flat-footin'" and "buck-dancing" in some areas. It is known for its freestyle movements. It can be a unique approach to aerobic exercise (if planned properly) because of its excellent physiological benefits.

The basic step is similar to a two-step (shuffle-ball-change or a triple-time step in the count of two). On count one, the weight is taken on the whole right foot. It is transferred to the

Figure 5-3. Clogging is a traditional form of square dancing that is usually performed to hoedown music.

ball of the left foot (on "and"). It returns to the whole right foot on count two. This basic footwork pattern is stylized then for clogging by adding a "brush forward" at the beginning of the step and keeping the knees loose (lifting alternately) throughout the basic. The pattern is repeated to the left, starting with a "brush forward" of the left foot. The sequence is continued.

A popular method of simplifying the basic step for beginners is to have them perform a shuffle-step first in which the toe of the foot is quickly brushed forward and then backward before the flat foot assumes the body weight. The knee of this leg bends as it receives the weight and then straightens as the other foot repeats the shuffle-step (also called Singles). Doubles consists of a quick-step (or a smooth rock-step). It is added to the shuffle-step to become the basic step originally discussed. The main advantage of this method is that the

Singles and Doubles may be performed as separate steps or in various combinations throughout the dance. The arms should swing freely at the sides or move forward (elbows bent slightly outward) in time with the music. Duple-time (2/4) hoedown (Country or Bluegrass) music is traditionally recommended for clogging. A slow version should be selected at first so as to allow beginners to become accustomed to fast-moving steps. Variations to the basic steps include kicks and wings, crosses, stomps, skips, and many other examples of fancy footwork. In some parts of the United States, this type of dancing is used as a "get-a-long" in traditional square dances and it also is used as a replacement for "fast dancing" (couple-style) at country socials (day or night). A modern style of clogging in which routines are performed in unison to contemporary "pop" music is gaining in popularity and adds a new flair to an old art.

Refer to Appendix C for more information on clogging basics.

Contras

Contras date back to the early beginnings of this country, but have found resurgence in recent times. They are performed in lines and circles and should be used as a learning device for either traditional or uncomplicated contemporary square dance calls. The dancers will gain confidence sooner because of the repetitive nature and the emphasis on musical timing in this versatile style of "longways" dancing. The music chosen should have a strong eight-count phrasing in the form of a hoedown, jig or reel. A prompter or caller usually stands at the head of the many-couple set(s) with the men on the prompter's right and the women on the left — with partners facing straight across; this formation is called "proper in a way." Another formation used is that of consecutive mini-squares with adjacent couples facing. The prompt is given during the latter part of the previous phrase. The music should allow plenty of time for the dancers to complete the movement. The basics are usually performed in the same manner as in square dancing (with the exception of the Allemande Left which is styled with an elbow hook or pigeon-wing). Contras also serve as mixers.

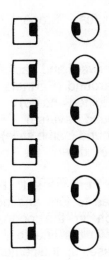

Figure 5-4. Contra dancing — "Proper in a Way" line formation.

0 X 0 Contra

Formation: six couples, "proper in a way." Call below includes instructions.

Call: First couple down the center (chassé with small sliding steps to the foot of the set)
Last couple up the outsides (of their own line, moving simultaneously with the head couple)
Do it again (to original position)
0 X 0 (the two outside sets of four Circle to the left and the center four Star by the right)
And back to place (reverse—outsides Circle right, centers Star left)
Everybody forward and back (in original lines)
Face the music (or prompter) and cast off to the foot
(All gents follow lead gent to the left, ladies to the right)
Make an arch (Head couple joins raised hands for a double arch)
All go under (New Head couple leads with chassés to top of set)

Virginia Reel

Formation: six couples, "proper in a way." Call below includes instructions.

Call: Everybody Forward and Back
Right hand around (Partners complete one turn with right hands joined and up)
Left hand around (reverse)
Both hand around (same style)
Head couple down the center and back (with chassés)
Head couple "reel the set" (Hook right elbows in the center so as to turn and hook left elbows with the next person in the opposite line; continue this pattern down the line to the foot of the set; head couple chassés up the center to the top of the set).
Cast off to the foot and form an arch (Refer to 0 X 0)

Big Circle Mountain Dancing

This type of square dance originated in the mountains of the Southeast. It requires a big ring of couples who are designated as "actives" or odd-numbered couples who lead to their right (counterclockwise) to perform Small Circle figures with the couples designated as "inactive" or even-numbered. The caller usually participates as an "active" and prompts or gives the commands which are usually simple, repetitious figures. Big Circle figures and Small Circle figures are used spontaneously for variety. Traditional hoedown music is appropriate.

Big Circle Figures

Circle (Left, Right)
Circle Single File, Lady in the Lead
Grand Right and Left
Swing
Promenade.

(King's, Queen's) Highway — Start with a partner Promenade in Line of Direction (counterclockwise). The designated lead couple man (King) or lady (Queen) promenades single file on the outside of the ring to travel in

Reverse Line of Direction (clockwise) while the partner continues in the original direction. Subsequently, every couple in order repeats the movement so as to follow the example of the lead couple. When partners meet again from opposite directions, they Promenade together.

London Bridge — Start with a partner Promenade in Line of Direction. Then the lead couple turns back 1/2 to make an arch with the inside arms and moves forward in Reverse Line of Direction. The next couple repeats the action and the lead couple immediately turns 1/2 again to go under the arches formed by the others. Promenade to "get out" of the figure.

Wind the Ball of Yarn — Start in a single circle with partners. The lead couple becomes the hub of a giant spiral of dancers that winds around them. To "get out," unwind the spiral in reverse.

Small Circle Figures

Formation: sets of one "active" and one "inactive" couple.

Birdie in the Cage
Take a Peek
Right Hands Across (Right Hand Star)
Left Hands Back (Left Hand Star)
Dive for the Oyster
Duck for the Clam
Lady Around the Lady
Lady Around the Gent
Various traditional figures

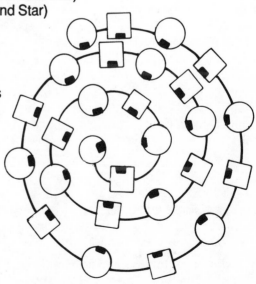

Figure 5-5. Wind the Ball of Yarn.

Part Three — Contemporary Square Dancing

Introduction

Until recent years, square dancing was limited to a few basic terms which could be learned quickly. But times have changed. Square dancing has evolved from the simple traditional style to a more complex system which is called the contemporary style. Here, the beginner learns a number of basic movements which are then expanded into a variety of patterns. These can be incorporated into either hash dancing or singing calls in which the melody and the music correspond to modern trends.

The Basic Movements of contemporary square dance have been divided into three categories: Basic Movements for One Couple, Basic Movements for Two Couples and Basic Movements for Four Couples. This classification system encourages a gradual degree of difficulty and will simplify the learning process.

The suggested hash practice calls and singing calls given in this section are only a few of many possible selections. They were chosen because of their application toward the practice of specific Basic Movements and their simplicity. The singing calls were selected because they have a good beat and/or a familiar melody so that dancers would find them fun. Some are duplicates from classic songs that will continue to stay in style. All of the recordings of the singing call drills in this section should be available at the source indicated at the end of each drill. If, for some reason a song is not obtainable, the suggested singing call should be used as another type of drill for practicing certain Basic Movements. Refer to Appendix A for a detailed description of the suggested singing calls.

Chapter six

Basic Movements
for One Couple

Some Basic Movements involving two dancers or one couple have been introduced previously in Chapter Three as the rudiments of all square dance. These include: Forward and Back, Do Sa Do, Allemande Family (Arm Swings) and Promenade Family. They should be reviewed again because they are mandatory in square dancing. Any of the Basic Movements for one couple can be practiced at home or wherever two people find it feasible. At this point, repetition is of utmost importance so that the novice dancer will learn to feel confident and natural while performing these fundamentals.

Half Sashay Family

Half Sashay. Starting in couple position, the partners simply exchange places without changing the direction they face. Both dancers take a side step toward each other, but the man will first step backward to allow the lady to pass him. He then steps sideward and forward to join hands on the other side.

Rollaway. This is a Half Sashay in which the dancer on the right rolls across with a full turn, passing in front of the partner who simply sidesteps to the right. The hands assist and initiate the movement with a slight pulling action.

(Reference note: To perform the call properly, Ladies In and Men Sashay, four couples are required. It is similar to a Half Sashay except it usually starts from a Circle to the Left, the ladies walk to the center and the men pass behind one lady to the left. The ladies return to rejoin hands with the men.)

44

Wheel Around

The couple makes a half turn (180 degrees) by the left hand dancer backing up while the right hand dancer moves forward. The central pivot point is located in between the handhold.

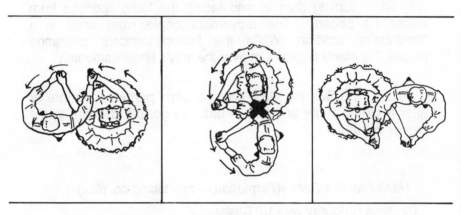

Figure 6-1. The Wheel Around .

California Twirl (Sometimes called Frontier Whirl)

The couple exchange places while turning 180 degrees. The joined hands are raised to form an arch through which the lady walks forward to make a half left face turn. Simultaneously, the man walks around the lady in a clockwise half turn. The couple maintains a loose handhold. They finish facing the opposite direction from which they started.

Figure 6-2. In the California Twirl, the two partners in a couple change places with each other while they move together to face the opposite direction.

Box the Gnat

Dancers face and extend right hands which are raised as the lady steps forward to do a left face underarm turn to end in the opposite position. The man simply walks forward around the lady while turning right to end facing the lady, opposite from where he began. The movement begins and ends in a handshake position. While the facing dancers exchange places, the man's fingers turn over the lady's fingers smoothly.

(Note: The Box the Gnat basic is often performed before or after a Grand Right and Left in order to get the dancers in the proper formation.)

Hash Practice Calls: (Formation — two facing couples)

Partners Rollaway with 1/2 Sashay
Box the Gnat with the opposite
Partners California Twirl
Partners Wheel Around and Promenade home

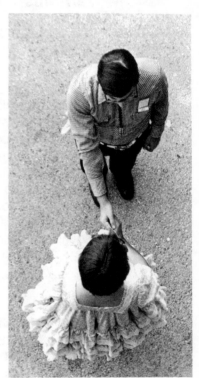

Figure 6-3. Box the Gnat.

Chapter seven

Basic Movements for Two Couples

In order to simplify the Basic Movements of square dance, there are some figures which only involve four dancers. These should be introduced in components of either two couple mini-squares or two active couples performing within the four couple conventional square. Using mini-squares of any two facing couples can save time and promote more activity, but often teachers prefer to use the conventional square to condition beginners for four couple dancing. Please repeat the drills or Hash Practice Calls with the Side couples if the conventional square formation is chosen.

Pass Thru

Opposites pass right shoulders and continue to face the original direction so that they will travel to each other's starting position. The man's right shoulder should be slightly forward as opposite dancers pass. The lady's right hand should lead with appropriate skirtwork while passing. Passing Rule — Always pass right shoulders to establish the right-of-way.

Drill: Head couples Pass Thru and California Twirl
Head couples Pass Thru and California Twirl (back home)

Refer to Appendix A for a Singing Call involving a Pass Thru —"Jackson," Kalox #K-1079, Caller — Billy Lewis; original recording performed by Johnny Cash.

Figure 7-1. Pass Thru movement of opposite couples. (*Photo courtesy of New England Square Dance Caller Magazine*, Lowell, Massachusetts.)

Turn Back Family

In a U-turn Back, the dancers make one-half turn in place to face the opposite direction.

Drill: Head couples Pass Thru and U-turn back
Repeat back to starting position

Back-track. Another form of a Turn Back is a Back-track. Couples can Back-track in Promenade position by turning one-half turn toward each other without releasing hands. A single dancer can Back-track, usually from a circle formation, by stepping outside the circle to face the opposite direction.

Separate Family

The couple turns back-to-back to walk around the outside perimeter of the square.

Separate —They travel any distance specified by the caller.

Divide —They travel 1/4 of the outside area of the square and await the next call.

Hash Practice Calls:

Heads Pass Thru
U-turn Back
Pass Thru
Separate around one
Into the middle
U-turn Back
Allemande Left
Partner Promenade

Refer to Appendix A for a simple, old-time Singing Call involving a Separate — "Solomon Levi," MacGregor #2003.

Split Family

The couples are facing so that the active inside couple moves between the inactive outside couple (maneuvering to allow the inside couple to pass through).   This involves "posting" in a four couple square; the inactives act as "posts." The actives perform the "gridwork" or movement around the "posts."

Split the Outside Couple. This movement is done from a starting formation of two facing couples.

Split the Ring. This movement is done in a square and only one couple is active.

Hash Practice Calls: (Formation: a four couple square would be preferable, but not mandatory)

Heads Pass Thru, Separate go around one
Go down the middle and Pass Thru, Split the outsides
And go around one, go down the middle and Pass Thru
California Twirl at home

Refer to Appendix A for a Singing Call involving a Pass Thru, Separate or Divide, etc.—"Cindy Balance," Blue Star BS #1508-A, Caller — Andy Andrus.

Right and Left Thru

Facing couples step forward to join right hands with the opposite dancer, then pull by. The partners then execute a fdjsfdsfdf

Courtesy Turn (leading with the left hand). They finish facing the same couple with whom they have exchanged positions.

Drill: Head couples Right and Left Thru across
Repeat back to starting position

Hash Practice Calls:

Heads Pass Thru
Separate around two
Hook on the ends (lines)
Go Forward and Back
Pass Thru, U-turn Back
Right and Left Thru
Allemande Left the corner

Refer to Appendix A for a Singing Call involving a Right and Left Thru, etc. ("Grand Square," Sets in Order #SIO F102A, Caller — Bob Osgood). The call, Grand Square, is also an important Basic Movement of square dance and is explained and illustrated as part of the teaching procedure for this Singing Call dance. It is initiated with a two couple formation and is then developed into a four couple formation. An excellent follow-up dance for Grand Square is also found in Appendix A ("Charlie's Polka," Kalox #K1151, Caller — Vaughn Parrish).

Square Thru Family (One — Four Hands)

A Square Thru is similar to a Right and Left Grand except the Square Thru is done in a mini-square formation with two facing couples. The sequence starts with the opposites joining right hands across and pulling by to face out. To continue, they make a 1/4 (90 degrees) turn inward to face the next person in the foursome (who is the starting partner) with whom they join left hands to pull by. This completes a Half Square Thru (two hands) and the dancers are facing the direction where the outside couples would be located. Next, they turn inward 1/4 turn to face the opposite and pull by with right hands. This completes a Three-Quarter Square Thru (three hands). To finish the (full) Square Thru, they turn inward 1/4 again to face the starting partner and pull by with left hands to face the direction where the outside couples would be located or where the starting corner is positioned. The call, Square Thru, could be shortened by the designated opposite couples walking forward to meet in the center and then making 1/4 turn to face the corner (the author calls this a square-off).

Hash Practice Calls:

Example 1:

Head couples Square Thru three hands
California Twirl with your girl

Example 2:

Head couples Square Thru
Split two around one
Line up four
Forward 8 and 8 fall back
Allemande Left the corner

(Note: Callers will sometimes have the dancers perform a Left Square Thru which starts with the left hand and continues with alternating hands accordingly. This leaves the left hand free at the completion of the call.)

Refer to Appendix A for Singing Calls involving a Square Thru: ("Gone at Last," Chaparral #C-301, Caller — Gary Shoemake; original recording performed by Johnny Paycheck. Also, "What It Means to be Blue," Kalox #K-1244, Caller — C.O. Guest).

Star Thru

Facing dancers place the man's right hand to the lady's left hand (palm to palm with the fingers pointing upward) to form an arch (well above the lady's head) under which the lady completes a 1/4 (90 degrees) left face turn. The man simultaneously walks around behind the lady to complete a 1/4 (90 degrees) turn to the right. They end the move facing a new direction, side by side, in couple position.

(Note: A Slide Thru is the same movement except no hands are used.)

Hash Practice Calls: (Note: Four Star Thrus or Slide Thrus or any combination thereof will return the couples to their home positions.)

Example 1:

Head couples Star Thru twice
Head couples Right and Left Thru across

Example 2:

Head couples Square Thru
Then Star Thru the outside two
California Twirl, U-Turn Back
Star Thru, California Twirl
Allemande Left the corner

Refer to Appendix A for a Singing Call involving a Star Thru, etc. ("Pecos Promenade," Chaparral #C-406, Caller— Beryl Main; original recording performed by Tanya Tucker)

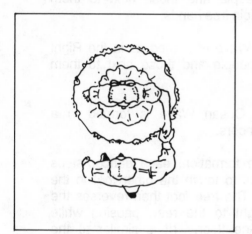
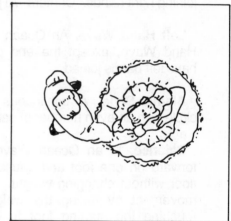

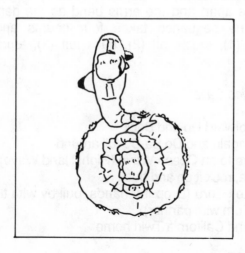

Figure 7-2. Star Thru.

Ocean Wave Family

Mini-waves consist of two dancers facing opposite directions with their arms bent at the elbows and hands joined about shoulder level to form a "W" in hands-up position. An Ocean Wave consists of 1 1/2, 2 or more Mini-waves in which three or more people are facing opposite directions from that of adjoining dancers.

Right Hand Wave. An even number of dancers form an Ocean Wave with the end people and those next to them joining right hands. Centers will join free hands.

Left Hand Wave. An Ocean Wave is formed as in the Right Hand Wave, except the end people and those next to them have left hands joined.

Alamo Style. A continuous Ocean Wave is formed in a circle with an even number of dancers.

Balance. In an Ocean Wave formation, each dancer steps forward on one foot and pauses to touch the other foot to the floor without changing weight. The free foot then reverses the movement by taking the weight to the rear, pausing while touching the starting foot to the floor. (It is similar to the Charleston basic step.) The arms extend forward as the dancers move apart and the arms bend as the dancers move together. The sequence takes four counts and is cued: forward right (1), touch left (2), back left (3), touch right (4). Repeat.

Hash Practice Calls:

Heads go Forward Up and Back
Go forward again and Do Sa Do full around
And 1/4 more to an Ocean Wave (Right Hand Wave)
And Balance, rock it up and back
Right and Left Thru (Drop left hands, pull by with the right and
   Courtesy Turn with partner)
Pass Thru and California Twirl home

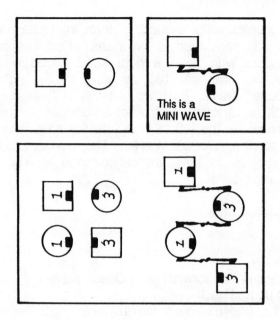

Figure 7-3. Right Hand Ocean Wave.

Pass the Ocean

Facing couples Pass Thru and make 1/4 turn inward to face the partner (equivalent to the floor pattern of a Star Thru) and then step into a Right Hand Ocean Wave.

Hash Practice Calls:

Example 1:

Head couples Pass the Ocean
Balance up and back
Right and Left Thru
Star Thru back home

Example 2:
Heads Promenade 1/2
Pass the Ocean
Pass Thru
Allemande Left the corner

Swing Thru Family

Facing couples step forward to form an Ocean Wave. A Swing Thru is performed in two parts. Part one consists of those dancers who have a right hand joined with another dancer turning one-half (180 degrees) by the right to form another Ocean Wave. Part two consists of those dancers who have a left hand joined with another dancer turning one-half (180 degrees) by the left to complete the sequence and they finish in another Ocean Wave. The dancers should hold elbows in close as they are called upon to weave moving forward along the line.

Hash Practice Calls:

Example 1:

Head couples step forward to an Ocean Wave
Balance up and back
Swing Thru (those who can turn 1/2 by the right, those
   who can then turn 1/2 by the left)
Swing Thru again
Right and Left Thru back home

Example 2:

Four Ladies Chain 3/4
Sides Square Thru 2 hands
Step to an Ocean Wave
Double Swing Thru (twice)
Pass Thru
Allemande Left the corner
Partner Promenade

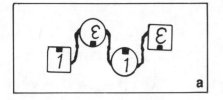

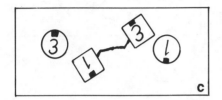

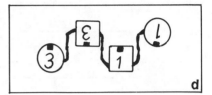

Figure 7-4. Right Swing Thru.

Left Swing Thru. Specifically called, the Left Swing Thru is the reverse of a regular Swing Thru. Those dancers who can, turn one-half by the left and those dancers who can, turn one-half by the right.

Alamo Swing Thru. From a circle, everyone simultaneously turns one-half by the right and then one-half by the left. (This procedure is reversed if a Left Swing Thru in Alamo Style is called.) Often a balance is inserted between the half-turns.

Trade Family

A Trade starts from a wave, line or column formation. It consists of two specific dancers or couples who exchange places by moving forward in a semicircle to assume the other dancer's starting position in the same line. They finish facing the opposite direction from which they started.

Boys, girls, ends, centers and partners can Trade. They should use hands-up position when adjacent opposite dancers face each other.

Couples Trade is called when the couple is to act as one complete unit and they exchange places with another couple in the same line. They should use the normal couple position throughout the movement.

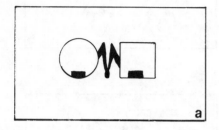
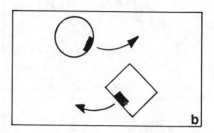

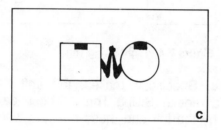

Figure 7-5. Partner Trade.

Hash Practice Calls:

Example 1:

Heads step forward to an Ocean Wave
Boys Trade, Girls Trade
Ends Trade, Centers Trade
Right and Left Thru
Pass Thru and California Twirl at home

Example 2:

Head Pass Thru
Partner Trade (repeat with Heads or with sides)

Refer to Appendix A for a Singing Call involving an Ocean Wave, Swing Thru and Trade ("Folsom Prison," Rockin A #1341, Caller— Roger Hopper; original recording performed by Johnny Cash).

Run Family

Formations are composed of two dancers who are side-by-side and facing either the same or opposite directions. The designated dancer walks forward in a semicircle and around the inactive dancer's other side. The latter (inactive dancer) fills the vacated place by taking a small step sideward without changing the facing direction. As a result, only the active dancer has changed to face the opposite direction.

Boys, girls, ends and centers can Run.

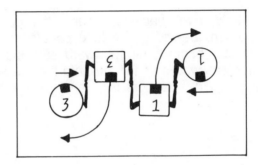

Figure 7-6. Boys Run.

Hash Practice Calls:

Example 1:

Heads Do Sa Do full around to an Ocean Wave
Double Swing Thru (Two Swing Thrus)
Girls Trade
Boys Run
Promenade your Partner home

Example 2:

Promenade (don't slow down)
All four couples Wheel Around
All four Boys Run
Turn partner by the Right
Allemande Left the corner

(Note: If a Cross Run is called, the two designated dancers criss-cross — right hand dancer in front, left hand dancer to the rear — and then Run to fill the other's place.)

Refer to Appendix A for a Singing Call involving Double Swing Thru and a Run ("American the Beautiful," Gold Star #GS 715, Caller—Cal Golden).

Zoom

The starting formation consists of a lead couple (or a single dancer) and a following couple (or a single dancer), one behind the other, facing the same direction.

Zoom is simply a roll back to assume the position of the couple (or person) behind. The lead couple separates (the single dancer rolls back) turning outward 360 degrees around the trailing persons who step forward into the position that has been vacated. The dancers will end facing the original direction.

Hash Practice Calls:

Heads Star Thru
Heads Zoom
Sides Zoom
Heads Square Thru three hands
Allemande Left the corner
Partner Promenade

Touch 1/4

Facing dancers move forward to the left so as to touch right hands, palm to palm, with fingers pointing upward. The dancers proceed to add a 1/4 (90 degree) turn without stopping.

Hash Practice Calls:

Example 1:

Heads Touch 1/4
Head boys Run right
Allemande Left the corner
Partner Promenade

Example 2:

Men Star Left (full)
Meet your partner
Touch 1/4
Boys Run
Allemande Left the corner

Veer Family

A Veer can be performed from a starting position of facing couples, facing single dancers, mini-waves or two-faced lines.

Veer Left or Veer Right. Two facing couples (or single dancers) move as a unit to the indicated direction and forward to form a two-faced line (or a mini-wave for single dancers).

(Note: If starting from a two-faced line or a mini-wave, the dancers move forward and inward toward the center of the line so as to end with the dancers back to back.)

 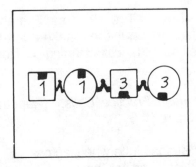

Figure 7-7. Veer Left.

Hash Practice Calls:

Example 1:

Head couples Right and Left Thru
Then Veer Left
And Veer Right
California Twirl back home

Example 2:

Heads Pass the Ocean
Then Swing Thru
Boys Run, Veer Right
Pass the Ocean
Swing Thru
Girls U-turn Back
Veer Left, Partner Trade
Star Thru, Allemande Left

Flutterwheel Family

A Flutterwheel starts with couples facing. The dancers on the right meet with a full right forearm turn in the center. As they meet the opposite inactive dancers, the latter are added to make a two-faced turning line. They remain in the Flutterwheel until they reach the original right hand dancer's starting position. The forearms in the center are then released and the new couples wheel in to face the center.

(Note: The Reverse Flutterwheel is the same except the dancers on the left make a left forearm turn and proceed to the left hand dancer's starting position.)

Hash Practice Calls: (Repeat with Side couples if using full square.)

Heads Flutterwheel across
Head Ladies Chain
Heads Right and Left Thru back home

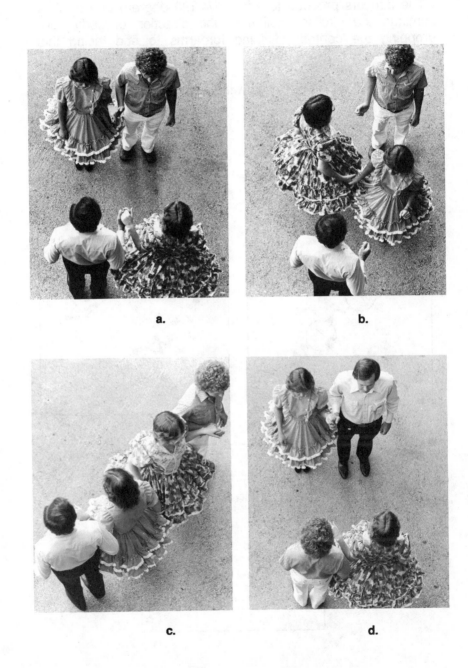

a.

b.

c.

d.

Figure 7-8. Flutterwheel Family.

Sweep 1/4

The dancers proceed to add a 1/4 (90 degree) turn as they continue the circling motion in the direction of body flow, dropping the central adjoining forearms to end facing that couple.

Hash Practice Calls: (Repeat with Side couples.)

Heads Flutterwheel
Heads Sweep 1/4
Heads Pass Thru
Allemande Left the corner
Partner Promenade

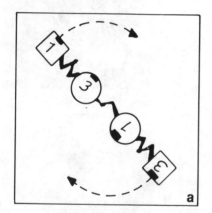

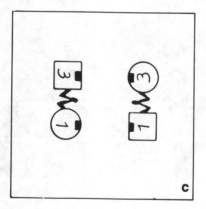

Figure 7-9. Diagram of Sweep 1/4 movement.

Chapter eight

Basic Movements
Requiring All Four Couples

The following Basic Movements involve the active partici-pation of all eight dancers in the square. The primary forma-tions used will be lines, columns, stars and circles. The hash practice calls usually require a "set-up and get-out" so that the left hand will be free for an Allemande Left to the corner and a partner Promenade. The Singing Calls involving specific Basic Movements are an integral part of the learning process and should be referred to in the Appendixes as suggested in the text. Both types of Calls serve only as good examples of the many others that could have been included. New Hash and Singing Calls are being developed and recorded continually. (*The American Square Dance Magazine* in Huron, Ohio is a good reference for new material.)

Lead Right

Starting in couple position, the specified dancers move forward and 90 degrees to the right to face directly the couple stationed there.

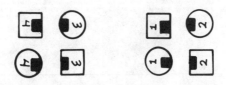

Figure 8-1. Diagram of Lead Right formation.

Circle to a Line

Facing couples Circle one-half. The leading person then drops the left handhold and becomes the left end portion of the line. The released person becomes the right end portion of the line by moving forward under an arch usually formed by the two right end dancers in the line. Keep the line straight.

Hash Practice Calls: (Circle to a Line)

The Route
(Old-time figure)

One and three you Bow and Swing
Then head right out to the right of the ring
Circle up four, you're doing fine
Head men break and form a line
Forward eight and back with you
Forward again and Right and Left Thru
Turn on around and Right and Left back
Two Ladies Chain across the set
Down the line two Ladies Chain (within the line)
Across the set two Ladies Chain.
Down the line two Ladies Chain (within the line)

Figure 8-2a. Circle to a Line.

Figure 8-2 b & c. Circle to a Line.

Wheel and Deal Family

A Wheel and Deal from a line of four dancers facing the same direction starts with the couple on the right (inside hands joined) wheeling inward (counterclockwise) toward the center of the line to face the opposite direction. The couple on the left (having stepped forward) wheels inward (clockwise) behind the other couple so that both couples face the same direction (double-file). On the Wheel Around, the center dancers act as a pivot point.

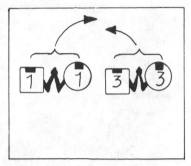

Figure 8-3. Wheel and Deal.

A Wheel and Deal from a two-faced line of four requires each couple to take one step forward and wheel inward toward the center to face the opposite direction. The couples end this sequence facing each other.

Hash Practice Calls:

Example 1: (standard)

Side Ladies Chain
Head couples Lead to the Right
Head men break to a line
Pass Thru
Wheel and Deal
Center two Square Thru three hands
Left Allemande the corner

Example 2: (two-faced line of four)

Head couples Square Thru
Swing Thru, Boys Run
Wheel and Deal
Allemande Left the corner

Refer to Appendix A for a Singing Call involving a Wheel and Deal from a two-faced line of four ("Hello, Mary Lou," Roadrunner #RR-302, Caller — Jerry Story with a revised and revived version; original recording performed by Rick Nelson).

Double Pass Thru

Two double-file sets of two couples (each set facing toward the center) move forward to pass right shoulders with two single-file dancers. Each set will end the sequence facing out.

Hash Practice Calls:

Example 1:

Heads Lead Right and Circle to a Line; go Forward Up and Back
Go Forward again and Pass Thru
Wheel and Deal (couple on the right wheels in first)
Double Pass Thru first couple go left, the next go right (to form a line again) and do a Right and Left Thru (if more practice is desired, alternate with a Pass Thru at this point)
Square Thru four hands (the "set-up and get-out" call)
Allemande Left the corner and partner Promenade

Example 2:

Head couples Star Thru
Double Pass Thru
Partner Trade
Double Pass Thru
Lead couple California Twirl
Allemande Left the corner

Refer to Appendix A for a Singing Call involving a Double Pass Thru, plus other previous calls ("Patriotic Medley," Blue Star #2025, Callers — Helt and Wykoff).

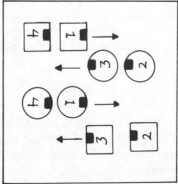

Figure 8-4. Diagram of the Double Pass Thru.

Bend the Line (or Go on to the Next)

A line with an even number of dancers is broken in half so that the centers move backward and the ends move forward to face the other half of the line.

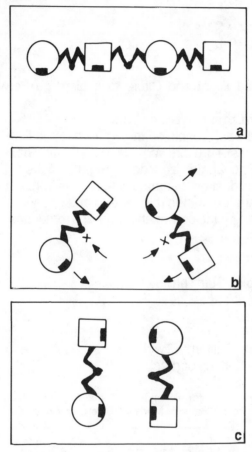

Figure 8-5. Diagram of Bend the Line (or Go on to the Next).

Cross Trail Thru

Facing couples Pass Thru (right shoulders) and proceed to criss-cross so that the right hand dancer crosses to the left in front of the left hand dancer who crosses to the right behind the partner. As the dancers cross, the leading shoulder is slightly forward. Any similar crossing calls will follow the Crossing Rule exemplified by this Basic Movement.

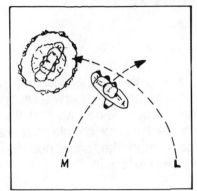

Figure 8-6. Diagram of the Cross Trail Thru.

Hash Practice Calls: (for a Two Couple Cross Trail Thru)

Example 1:

Heads Right and Left Thru
Side couples Cross Trail Thru to the corner
Allemande Left and partner Promenade (Repeat with
  alternating couples)

Example 2:

Heads Right and Left Thru
Heads Square Thru
Split two round one
Into the middle
Cross Trail Thru
Allemande Left the corner

Hash Practice Calls: (for a Four Couple Cross Trail Thru)

Promenade and don't slow down.
Head couples Wheel Around (180 degrees turn to form two
  lines of four)
Everyone Pass Thru (to face out)
Bend the Line (to be in position for a Cross Trail, corner must
  be located on the ends of the same line and straight across
  from each other in the centers of the line. After the Cross
  Trail, the corner will be met on the outsides for the centers
  and on the insides for the ends.)
Cross Trail Thru
Allemande Left the corner

Dive Thru

As couples are facing, the inside couple (whose back is to the center of the square, unless otherwise specified) makes an arch with their inside hands joined so that the outside couple can duck under the arch. The couple that made the arch is facing out and completes the sequence by performing an automatic California Twirl to face in.

Hash Practice Calls:

Example 1:

Head couples Square Thru two hands (to face the Sides)
Right and Left Thru
Dive Thru (automatic California Twirl for those facing out)
Pass Thru (centers only)
Allemande left the corner
Partner Promenade

Example 2:

Heads Square Thru (four hands)
Right and Left Thru
Dive Thru
Square Thru three hands
Allemande Left the corner
Partner Promenade

Trade By

The dancers must be in a starting formation of two couples facing in the center and two couples facing out on the ends of the two columns formed. The two facing couples Pass Thru while the other two couples complete a Partner Trade to end facing in.

Hash Practice Calls:

Example 1:

Heads Square Thru two hands
Right and Left Thru with the outside two
Pass Thru
Trade By
Allemande Left the corner
Partner Promenade

Example 2:

Heads Lead Right and Circle to a Line
Square Thru (four hands)
Trade By
Square Thru three hands
Trade By
Square Thru three hands
Allemande Left the corner
Partner Promenade

Refer to Appendix A for Singing Calls involving a Trade By ("Dream Lover," Rhythm #RR-150, Caller— Wade Driver with a revised and revived version; original recording performed by Bobby Darin; "Good Hearted Woman," Rhythm #RR-119, Caller—Wade Driver and Pat Barbour; original recording by Waylon Jennings and Willie Nelson).

Figure 8-7. Thar Family movements.

Thar Family

Allemande Thar. A star formation that may be assumed at the end of a left arm swing is known as an Allemande Thar. The center dancers form a right hand packsaddle star (also known as a box star) which travels backwards. The outside dancers walk forward using a left forearm grip with the center dancers.

Hash Practice Calls:

Four men Right Hand Star
Turn partner left to an Allemande Thar
Men back up...all let go; move up to corner
Allemande Left the corner
Partner Promenade

Wrong Way Thar. This call is the reverse of an Allemande Thar. It can occur at the end of any right arm turn involving the center dancers.

Hash Practice Calls:

Four men Right Hand Star
Turn partner by the left
Get the corner for a Wrong Way Thar
Men back in for a Left Hand Star
Drop hands, move up to partner
Do Sa Do and Promenade

Shoot the Star (half, full)

From either Thar formation, the center dancers break their handhold from the Star and make one-half arm turn with the outside dancer (unless otherwise directed as in a full turn).

Hash Practice Calls:

Allemande Left and an Allemande Thar
Go right and left and make a Star
Back it up Boys (right hand lady)
Shoot the Star (1/2 turn) to the Heaven's whirl
Go right and left to the second girl
Back it up Boys (corner).
Shoot the Star; find your maid (partner)
Take her by the hand and Promenade (back home)

Refer to Appendix A for Singing Calls involving an Allemande Thar and Shoot the Star a full turn ("Oblah-Di, Oblah-Da," Top #25198, Caller — Dick Leger; original recording by the Beatles. Also, "Fever," Windsor #5013, Caller — Nate Bliss; original recording performed by Peggy Lee, Elvis Presley, and others).

Slip the Clutch

From either Thar formation, the center dancers stop traveling backward, release the outside dancers so that everyone now moves forward in the same floor pattern as before (two single-file facing circles).

Do Paso

This call is a figure-eight sequence involving a one-half (180 degrees) left arm swing with the partner, then a one-half (180 degrees) right arm swing with the corner and a Courtesy Turn with the starting partner to "square-up" or to await the next call when the partners are reunited.

Hash Practice Calls:

Allemande Left and Allemande Thar
Go right and left and make a Star
Back it up Boys
Shoot the Star and away we go
With a right and left, then Do Paso her by the left (original corner), corner by the right (original Opposite), her by the left with a full turn around (original Corner), men go in for another Thar
Back it up Boys
Slip the Clutch (everyone moves forward); pass one; pass another; pass Mother
Allemande Left (corner) and partner Promenade

Circulate Family

Starting from waves, columns, lines or two-faced lines, all of the Circulate figures require specific dancers to move forward along the Circulate path (in a modified circle) to the next position.

Boys, girls, ends and centers can be directed to Circulate. Sometimes two groups will be asked to Circulate simultaneously.

Wave or Line
Circulate Path

Couples
Circulate Path

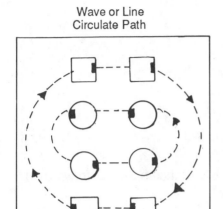
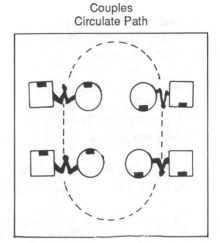

Figure 8-8. Diagram of Circulate Family movements.

Hash Practice Calls:

Example 1:

Head couples Square Thru four hands (face the sides)
Do Sa Do full around and 1/4 More to an Ocean Wave
Balance up and back
Boys Circulate (the outsides or ends are facing in a clockwise
circle and move up to the next position regardless of line)
Girls Circulate (the insides of centers are facing in a counter
clockwise circle and move up to the next position
regardless of line)
Ends Circulate (same as for Boys — take the next position)
Centers Circulate (same as for Girls — take the next position)
Right and Left Thru (pull by with the right hand and Courtesy
Turn)
Dive Thru
Square Thru three hands
Allemande Left and partner Promenade

Example 2:

Heads Square Thru
Swing Thru, Balance
Girls Circulate
Boys Circulate
All Eight Circulate
Swing Thru, Balance
Right and Left Thru
Allemande Left

Note: **Couples Circulate** — two dancers move forward in the circular position simultaneously.

Refer to Appendix A for Singing Calls involving: (1) All Eight Circulate, Double Swing Thru ("Rocky Top," Kalox #K-1115, Caller — Allen Tipton; performed by many country recording artists); (2) Couples Circulate, Allemande Thar, Star Thru, Swing Thru, Boys Run, Wheel and Deal, Dive Thru, etc. ("Golden Rocket," Gold Star #701, Caller — Cal Golden; original recording performed by Hank Snow).

Compound Circulates. A Box Circulate, Single File Circulate (in columns), and a Split Circulate (from lines, waves or columns) each has two separate formations acting independently of each other.

Hash Practice Calls: (Single File Circulate)

Heads Lead Right and Circle to a Line
Touch 1/4
Single File Circulate
Boys Run
Allemande Left the Corner

Hash Practice Calls: (Box Circulate)

Head Ladies Chain
Touch 1/4 (heads)
Box Circulate (heads)
Boys Run
Pass Thru
Allemande Left the corner

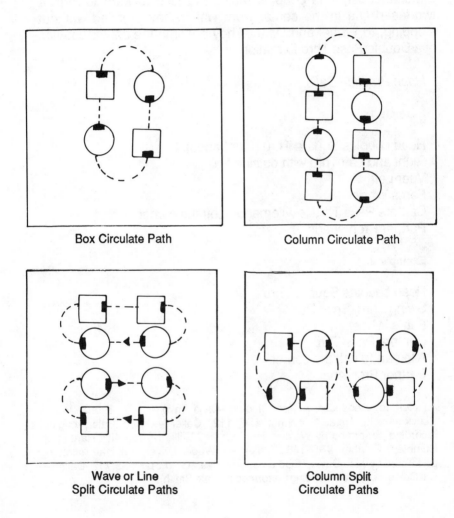

Box Circulate Path

Column Circulate Path

Wave or Line
Split Circulate Paths

Column Split
Circulate Paths

Figure 8-9. Diagram of Compound Circulate Movements.

Ferris Wheel

One two-faced line is parallel to another two-faced line so as to allow the couples facing out to Wheel and Deal to become the outside couples in a Double Pass Thru position. Simultaneously, the couples facing in move forward to form a two-faced line in the center from which they proceed, without stopping, to Wheel and Deal. They become the center couples of a Double Pass Thru formation.

Hash Practice Calls:

Example 1:

Head couples Square Thru (four hands)
Right and Left Thru with outside two
Veer Left
Ferris Wheel
Centers Pass Thru to Allemande Left the corner
Partner Promenade

Example 2:

Head couples Square Thru
Swing Thru, Boys Run
Ferris Wheel
Centers Pass Thru
Allemande Left the corner
Partner Promenade

Refer to Appendix A for Singing Calls involving a Ferris Wheel ("Luckenbach, Texas," Rhythm #RR-112, Caller — Bob Baier; original recording performed by Waylon Jennings and Willie Nelson; "It's Hard to be Humble," Rhythm #RR-146, Caller — Wade Driver; original recording performed by Mac Davis; "God Bless America," Gold Star #GS 712, Caller — Cal Golden; original recording performed by Kate Smith).

Figure 8-10 a & b. Ferris Wheel.

Figure 8-10c. Ferris Wheel.

Figure 8-11. Diagram of Ferris Wheel movement.

Appendixes

APPENDIX A

CLASSIC EXAMPLES OF SUGGESTED SINGING CALL DRILLS

Note: If the suggested recording is unavailable: 1. The pattern should be used as another type of drill for practice. 2. Reset the pattern to other music. 3. The suggested singing calls are only a few of many possible selections which are released monthly.

Preliminary Calls. Note: The Grand March can be used for forming squares (especially with large groups).

Choose any good march music. Starting position is a circle of couples (man on the left). First, Circle to the left and reverse to the right, single file, the lady in the lead; Men move up (in couple position with the man on the left) and Promenade (counterclockwise).

Grand March: A predesignated couple breaks the circle to lead the other couples up the center of the hall. When the stage area is reached, the couples peel off with the first turning to the right, the second turning to the left, and they are followed by alternate couples. As they meet another couple at the back of the hall, they travel up the center in sets of four. Then these sets peel off again with the first turning to the right, the second turning to the left, and they are followed by alternate sets of two couples. When they meet at the back of the hall this time, it will be in sets of eight coming up the center of the hall. The Grand March is complete. Sets of eight will scatter to the right and left to Circle and then "square-up."

Simple, Old-time Singing Call:

"Marching Thru Georgia," Windsor #4112

Opener and Middle Break:

Bow to your partners and to your corners all
Join those hands and Circle Left, you Circle round the hall
Circle to the Right boys, the other way back home
Swing your partner 'cause that's the way we do it down in
  Georgia

Figure:

First old lady Promenade the inside of the ring
When you meet your old man just give him a great big Swing
Everybody turn to the right, Promenade single file (place
  right hand on the left shoulder of dancer in front)
Just the way they do it down in Georgia
Hip hip hurray, let's go the other way (reverse arms and
  direction of travel) — Hip hip hurray, go back the other way
  (reverse again)
When you get to your back door (home position)
Everybody Swing just like they do it down in Georgia

Simple, Old-time Singing Call: (this is a mixer to get
dancers acquainted)

" Oh, Johnny, Oh," Blue Star #1690

You all join hands and you Circle the ring
Stop where you are give your honey a Swing
Swing the girl behind you, Swing you own if you have time
Allemande Left the corner girl
Do Sa Do your own
Then you all Promenade with the sweet corner maid
Singing "Oh, Johnny, Oh, Johnny, Oh"

Simple, Old-time Singing Call:

"Comin' Round the Mountain," Windsor # 4115

Chorus:

Oh the Head couples Ladies Chain
Side couples Swing
Chain them round the mountain
Swing at home
Now the Side couples Ladies Chain
Head couples Swing again
Chain them round the mountain
Chain them home

Break:

Allemande Left your corner
Right hand to your own (pull by)
Swing the next lady on your right (new partner)
Swing her high and Swing her low
Hug her tight and around you go
And Promenade the mountain, Promenade
(Repeat three more times to return to original partner)

Suggested Singing Call Drill: (Formation — 4 couple square)

"Jackson," Kalox #K-1079, Caller — Billy Lewis; original recording performed by Johnny Cash.

Opener, Break, Ending:

Join sixteen hands and you Circle that ring
Going hotter than a pepper sprout
Hey Allemande Left the corner, come back you Do Sa Do
Those men Promenade inside (to the right inside the set)
All the way back to Jackson
Do Sa Do and Promenade
We're going back to Jackson
Just looking for a shade

Figure: (Repeat four times — each time the lady moves one position to the right and eventually returns "home.")

Four little Ladies Chain Three Quarters round you go
Those Heads (Sides) Promenade about Half way (outside)
Hey the Sides (Heads) Pass Thru, California Twirl you do
  (men are with corner in opposite position)
Left Allemande and Weave that Ring (back to corner)
All the way back to Jackson, Do Sa Do and Promenade
All the way back to Jackson, just looking for a shade

Sequence: Opener, Figure twice Heads, Break, Figure twice Sides, Ending.

Simple, Old-time Singing Call:

"Solomon Levi," MacGregor #2003 or other compatible
music

Hey the first old couple Separate
Go round the outside track
You meet your partner going round
You pass her coming back
Now honors to your corners
Salute your partners all
You Swing that pretty corner girl
And you Promenade the hall

(Note: This figure can be repeated with both head couples,
both side couples, or all four couples working simultaneously.)

Suggested Singing Call Drill: (Formation — conventional square)

"Cindy Balance," Blue Star #BS-1508-A, Caller — Andy Andrus

Opener:

Sashay (Do Sa Do) round the corner gal
Come back and Swing your own
Allemande Left the corner gal
   and Promenade Cindy Home (add patter calls and Swing)

Figure:

The two Head couples go down the middle, Split the Ring in
   two (same as Pass Thru, Separate)
Come in the open window (go around one) and Balance
   Cindy Lou (facing partner, Balance by stepping on left foot
   and hopping while swinging right foot forward and repeat
   to other side. Continue until the call changes).
Walk all around (Do Sa Do) old Cindy Lou and Swing her
   too (active couples are now in the opposite position)
Repeat with the two Side couples.

Break: (At its completion, the ladies will be with the corner)

Allemande Left the corner girl, Allemande Right your own
Go back and Swing the corner girl and Promenade her
   home

Sequence: Opener, Figure, (Heads once, Sides once), and
adjoining Break (repeat four times)

Suggested Singing Call Drill: (Formation — mini and conventional squares)

"Grand Square," Sets in Order #SIO F102A, Caller — Bob Osgood

Openers, Breaks, Closer:

The basic Grand Square pattern is used often in contemporary square dance. It should be taught first to the Head couples only, next the Side couples should learn their part and finally the two parts are combined to make a "Grand Square."

The Head couples are facing (their opposites) and take four steps forward to meet each other (starting with the right foot); on count 4, they turn 1/4 to face their partner and back up four steps (they are now in the Side positions with the opposite); on count 4, they turn 1/4 to face their original opposite and back up 4 steps; on count 4, they turn 1/4 to face their partner and they take four steps toward each other. On count 4, there is no 1/4 turn since the couples are back to their home positions. They simply place their palms together to push-off so as to reverse the procedure by backing up for the first four counts. Each person has a square foot pattern delineated on the floor one-half way through the sequence and again as it is reversed.

The Side Couples start facing their partner with palms together so that they can back up four counts (starting with the right foot) and they proceed with the same sequence as performed by the Head couples one-half way through on the reverse portion.

The two parts are then combined so that each dancer's small individual square becomes part of the large "Grand Square."

Figure: The same pattern is performed with these three basic movements.

First Chorus: Right and Left Thru
Second Chorus: Two Ladies Chain
Third Chorus: Couples Half Promenade and Right and Left back

The Chorus is performed in this manner:

Head couples complete the basic movement across the set and back. Side couples complete the basic movement across the set and back. Head couples face to the right (Side couple faces to the left) to form two diagonal lines across the set. The basic movement is then performed with the opposite couple and back again. Side couples face to the right (Head couples to the left) and repeat the basic movement across and back.

Sequence: Opener, Figure, Break, Figure, Break, Figure, Closer.

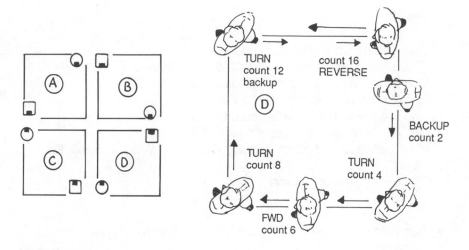

Figure A-1. Diagram of Grand Square (left) and exploded view of Dancer D, man's part (right).

Suggested Singing Call Drill: (Follow-up dance for Grand Square)

"Charlie's Polka," Kalox #K1151, Caller — Vaughn Parrish

Opener, Break, Ending:

Left Allemande and then your partner Swing
Join hands and Circle round the ring
All the way 'til you're home again (move quickly)
When you're there — Sides face, Grand Square —
Reverse — Would you, won't you, could I coax you
Come on you said you would, play that old piano for me

Figure:

Four Ladies Chain, turn 'em and then
Chain those ladies right back home again again
You join all your hands and Circle round that old land
Left Allemande and Weave the Ring
You Weave it in and out 'til you meet your maid
Do Si Do and take the Corner girl and Promenade
Play it sweet and keep it neat, Come on Charlie, keep that
 beat
Tickle that old ivory for me

Sequence:　　Opener, Figure twice, Break, Figure twice,
　　Ending

Suggested Singing Call Drill:

"Gone at Last," Chaparral #C-301, Caller — Gary Shoemake, original recording performed by Johhny Paycheck

Opener, Break, Ending:

Four ladies Promenade go inside the ring
Get back, Swing your man around
Join all of your hands, Circle left and then
Left Allemande that corner, Weave the Ring
Gone at last, gone at last, Do Sa Do, you Promenade
Around you go; I've had a long streak of that bad luck
But I pray it's gone at last

Figure:

Heads (Sides) Promenade half-way around
Two and Four (one and three) do a Right and Left Thru
Now Square Thru and go four hands around you go
Everybody Allemande and Weave the Ring
Gone at last, Gone at last, Do Sa Do, you Promenade
Around you go; I've had a long streak of that bad luck
But I pray it's gone at last

Sequence: Opener, Figure twice Heads, Break, Figure twice Sides, Ending

Suggested Singing Call Drill:

"What It Means to be Blue," Kalox #K-1244, Caller — C.O. Guest

Opener, Break, Ending:

Join all of your hands, start to Circle
Walk around the corner (Do Sa Do), See Saw the one you know
Those men Star Right, go once around tonight
Left Allemande then Weave that 'ol Ring
(lyrics) Swing and Promenade home

Figure:

Heads (Sides) Square Thru and get me four hands
And with the Sides (Heads) make a Right Hand Star
Now the Heads (Sides) Star by the Left, go once (in the center)
Do Sa Do the corner girl (same girl as before both Star figures)
Now Square Thru and count four hands around you go
To the corner Swing and Promenade
You Promenade by twos and I love only you
And I know what it means to be blue

Sequence: Opener, Figure twice Heads, Break, Figure twice Sides, Ending.

Suggested Singing Call Drill:

"Pecos Promenade," Chaparral #C-406, Caller — Beryl Main, original recording performed by Tanya Tucker.

Opener, Break, Ending:

Sides face, Grand Square
Circle to the left, Well you lead off with the Cotton-Eyed Joe,
   Buck and Wing and heel and toe
Left Allemande and Promenade now

Figure:

Well the Heads (Sides) you Promenade
Go about half way round the ring
Now Two and Four (One and Three) you do a Do Si Do
Star Thru, Pass Thru and Swing the corner round
Left Allemande and Weave the Ring
Do Sa Do and Promenade now

Sequence: Opener, Figure twice Heads, Break, Figure twice
   Sides, Ending

Tag: (Words to the song)

They may like to rock and roll in Dallas and Disco in
   Galveston Bay
But when God made those west Texas cowboys,
He gave them the Texas Promenade
Tonight was the first time I saw her,
We can still hear those twin fiddles play
Well, Houston starts to feel like a Lone Star Heaven
As we dance to that Pecos Promenade
Well the beer sign's hanging by the door, saw dust on that
   old dance floor, tip your hat for the Pecos Promenade

Suggested Singing Call Drill:

"Folsom Prison," Rockin A #1341, Caller — Roger Hopper; original recording performed by Johnny Cash

Intro, Break, Ending:

Allemande Left with the corner
Do Sa Do your own
Allemande Left just once again
And Weave around the Ring
Far from Folsom Prison, Do Sa Do and Promenade
Far from Folsom Prison, that's where I want to stay

Figure:

One and three Square Thru
Four hands around you go (to face the corner)
Do Sa Do the outsides
It's full around you know (step to an Ocean Wave)
Swing Thru two by two (one time)
Boys Trade (in the center) and Promenade (the corner)
And let that lonesome whistle blow your blues away

Sequence: Intro, Figure twice Heads, Break, Figure twice Sides, Ending.

Suggested Singing Call Drill:

"America The Beautiful," Gold Star #GS 715, Caller —
Cal Golden

Opener, Middle Break, Closer:

Four Ladies Chain 3/4 round you go
Join hands and Circle to the Left
Four Ladies Rollaway (1/2 Sashay)
Circle to the Left
Left Allemande the corner Weave the Ring
America, America Do Sa Do and Promenade
And crown thy good with brotherhood
From sea to shining sea

Figure:

Heads (Sides) Square Thru get me four hands you know
With the Sides you make a Right Hand Star
Heads in the middle make a Left Hand Star
Turn it one time (go back to face the corner)
Same Two you do the Right and Left Thru
Swing Thru and then, Swing Thru again
Boys Run to the Right and Promenade
And crown thy good with brotherhood
From sea to shining sea

Optional Middle Break:

Sides face, Grand Square:

I pledge allegiance to the flag of the United States
    of America, and to the republic for which it stands,
One nation, under God, indivisible with liberty
And justice for all; Circle left
America, America, Left Allemande and Promenade
And crown thy good with brotherhood
From sea to shining sea

Optional Closer:

Circle Left, Oh beautiful for spacious skies
For amber waves of grain, Left Allemande the corner
Turn the partner by the right and your corners Allemande
Come back Swing your partner Promenade
And crown thy good with brotherhood
From sea to shining sea

Sequence: Opener, Figure twice Heads, Middle Break, Figure twice Sides, Closer

Suggested Singing Call Drill:

"Hello Mary Lou," Roadrunner Records #RR-302, Caller — Jerry Story with a revised and revived version; original recording performed by Rick Nelson

Opener, Break:

Circle Left
Allemande Left, Weave around that Ring
Hey, Hey, Hello Mary Lou, goodbye heart
Do Sa Do and Promenade
I knew, Mary Lou, we'd never part
So Hello, Mary Lou, goodbye heart

Figure:

Heads (Sides) Square Thru four hands round you go
To the corner do a Do Sa Do
Swing Thru two by two, boys Run right
Wheel and Deal, pull 'em on around and now
Right and Left Thru, make a Right Hand Star 1/2
Girls turn back, Swing corner lady and Promenade

Ending:

Four ladies Promenade back home, Swing your man
Join hands Circle Left
Left Allemande, Weave the Ring

Sequence: Opener, Figure twice Heads, Break, Figure twice Sides, Ending

Suggested Singing Call Drill:

"Patriotic Medley," Blue Star #2025, Callers — Helt and Wykoff

Opener, Middle Break, Closer:

Circle Left, Yankee Doodle went to town a riding on a pony
Stuck a feather in his hat and called it macaroni
Allemande Left your corner, partner Box the Gnat
All the ladies Promenade once inside the set
Turn your partner by the right, full around you go
Allemande Left with the corner, come back and Promeno
Yankee Doodle keep it up, Yankee Doodle Dandy
Mind the music and the step and with the girls be handy

Figure:

One and Three (Two and Four) Promenade, go 1/2 way
  around the floor
Two and Four (One and Three) Pass Thru, around one make
  a line of four
Go Forward eight to the middle and come on Back
Star Thru, All Double Pass Thru
Lead couple Partner Trade, make a Right Hand Star
Go once around, Girls turn back and Swing, Promenade
Promenade with the lady fair, walk that gal around the square
Yes, we'll all be glad when Johnny comes marching home

Sequence: Opener, Figure — Heads, Sides, Middle Break

Figure: Sides, Heads, Closer

Song Line Variations:

Figures:

#2 — We are proud to claim the title of the U. S.
       Marines
#3 — We'll look up with hearts that are free and from
       afar we'll see Stars and Stripes forever
#4 — Keep your eye on the Grand Old Flag

Suggested Singing Call Drill:

"Dream Lover," Rhythm #RR-150, Caller — Wade Driver with a revised and revived version; original recording performed by Bobby Darin

Open, Break, Close:

Circle Left; Every night I hope and pray, a dream
Lover will come my way, Left Allemande, you'll Do Sa Do
Left Allemande, c'mon and Weave it you know
Because I want a girl, Do Sa Do and Promenade along
I want a dream lover so I won't have to dream alone

Figure:

Four Ladies Chain, three-quarters around
Head (Side) couples Promenade half-way around
Come down the middle gonna Square thru four
Go all the way and do the Right and Left Thru
C'mon and Pass Thru, Trade By, Left Allemande
Swing your lady, Promenade the land
I want a dream lover so I won't have to dream alone

Tag:

Sides face, Grand Square (16 beats only)
I want a dream lover so I won't have to dream alone

Sequence: Open, Figure twice Heads, Break, Figure twice Sides, Close, Tag.

Suggested Singing Call Drill:

Good Hearted Woman," Rhythm #RR-119, Callers — Driver and Barbour, original recording performed by Waylon Jennings and Willie Nelson

Open, Break, Close:

Sides face, Grand Square
A long time forgotten, are dreams that just fell by the way
The good life he promised, ain't what she's living today
Left Allemande, Weave the Ring
She never complains of the bad times or the bad things he's
    done
Do Sa Do and Promenade
She just talks about the good times they've had and all the
    good times to come

Figure:

Heads (Sides) Promenade and go 1/2 way around
You know, come down the middle and Square Thru four, four
    hands around and then
Right and Left Thru my friend
Turn the girl, Slide Thru (Star Thru without using hands)
You Square Thru again four hands around that ring now,
Trade By (insides Pass Thru, outsides partner Trade), the
    corner lady Swing
Swing that girl and Promenade
She's a good hearted woman in love with a good timing man

Sequence: Open, Figure twice Heads, Break, Figure twice Sides, Close

Additional Lyrics: Break and Close

Suggested Singing Call Drill:

"Oblah-Di, Oblah-Da," Top #25198, Caller — Dick Leger, original recording performed by the Beatles.

Intro, Break, Ending:

Allemande Left with a Allemande Thar,
Go forward two my friend
Go right and left and the men hang on,
Make a back up Star and then
Shoot that Star a full turn around (to the dancer with whom
    you started this part) with the "corner" Box the Gnat
Same little lady, Do Sa Do, then Weave the Ring like that

Chorus:

Oblah-Di, Oblah-Da, life goes on — hey
Do Sa Do and Promenade her home
Obla Dee, Obla Dah, life goes on — hey
Take that lady home and don't you roam

Figure:

Heads (Sides) Square thru four hands
In de market place
When you meet your corner lady Swing
Join your hands and Circle all around de place
Then you Allemande Left new corner, Weave the Ring
(Repeat Chorus)

Suggested Singing Call Drill:

"Fever," Windsor #5013, Caller — Nate Bliss, original recording performed by Peggy Lee, Elvis Presley, and others

Opener, Break, Closer:

Four Ladies Chain and you turn this girl
Circle to the left you go
You do an Allemande Left, go Allemande Thar
Go forward two and make a Star, she gives me fever
Shoot that Star and you Turn Thru (same as an Arm Swing)
Left Allemande and then you Promenade, fever's not a new
   thing,
Fever started a long time ago

Figure:

Heads (Sides) Promenade just half-way
Down the middle with a Right and Left Thru
Square Thru you know, Four hands you go
Do Sa Do with the outside two, you're gonna Swing Thru
Boys Trade and you Turn Thru (Arm Swing) to
Left Allemande and then you Promenade
Fever in the morning, fever all through the night

Sequence: Opener, Figure twice Heads, Break, Figure twice Sides, Closer

Suggested Singing Call Drill:

"Rocky Top," Kalox #K-1115, Caller — Allen Tipton, original recording performed by many country artists

Opener, Break, Ending:

Four Ladies Chain, go across that ring, now
Rollaway, Circle the ring
Four Ladies Rollaway (again), Circle the Ring, now
Left Allemande and Weave the Ring
Rocky Top you'll always be, Do Sa Do and Promenade
To good old Rocky Top, Rocky Top Tennessee

Figure:

Heads (Sides) Promenade go 1/2 way around, now
Down the middle and then Square Thru
Count four hands you go, Meet 'em there Do Sa Do
Back to back and Double Swing Thru
When you're there, All Circulate and Swing, Promenade to
   good old Rocky Top, Rocky Top Tennessee

Sequence: Opener, Figure twice Heads, Break, Figure twice Sides, Ending

Suggested Singing Call Drill:

"The Golden Rocket," Gold Star #GS 701, Caller — Cal Golden, original recording by Hank Snow

Opener, Break, Closer:

Four little Ladies Chain I say, 3/4 round in the usual way
Join hands and make a great big ring, Circle to the Left
Allemande Left, Allemande Thar
Go Right and Left and make a Star
Men back up and make a Right Hand Star
Shoot that Star full turn around
Slip the Clutch, Left Allemande
Come back and Promenade her home
I'm tired of runnin' on the same old track
Bought a one way ticket and I won't be back
This Golden Rocket is a rollin' my blues away

Figure:

One and Three Promenade 1/2 way round the ring I say
Down the middle and do a Right and Left Thru
Turn your girl, Star Thru, Pass Thru
Swing Thru, two by two, boys Run Right,
Couples Circulate, Wheel and Deal, Dive Thru
Square Thru 3/4 around and Swing that corner and
    Promenade
I want a good engine a runnin' on time
So Baby I'm switching to another line
This Golden Rocket is a rollin' my blues away

Sequence: Opener, Figure twice Heads, Break, Figure twice Sides, Closer

Suggested Singing Call Drill:

"Luckenbach, Texas," Rhythm #RR-112, Caller — Bob Baier, original recording performed by Waylon Jennings and Willie Nelson

Open, Break, Close:

Sides face, Grand Square
Let's go to Luckenbach, Texas, with Waylon and Willie and
   the boys
This successful life we're living's got us feudin'
Like the Hatfields and McCoys; Left Allemande,
Weave the Ring, Between those Hank Williams' pain songs
And Newberry's train songs, Do Sa Do and Promenade
Down in Luckenbach, Texas, there ain't nobody feelin' no
   pain

Figure:

Heads (Sides) Promenade and go, 1/2 way around you know
Come down the middle Square Thru Four
Four hands around and then, go Right and Left Thru my
   friend
Turn the girl, Veer to the Left, you Ferris Wheel and then
Centers Square Thru 3/4, Swing your Corner
One time around and Promenade
Down in Luckenbach, Texas there ain't nobody feelin' no
   pain

Sequence: Open, Figure twice Heads, Break, Figure twice
   Sides, Close

Suggested Singing Call Drill:

"It's Hard to be Humble,"   Rhythm #RR-146, Caller —
Wade Driver, original recording performed by Mac Davis

Open, Break, Close:

Sides face, Grand Square; Oh Lord, it's hard to be humble,
When you're perfect in every way
I can't wait to look in the mirror
I get better looking each day; Circle left
To know me is to love me, Left Allemande, Promenade
Oh Lord, it's hard to be humble
But I'm doing the best that I can

Figure:

Heads (Sides) Square Thru, count me four hands
With the corner lady do a Do Sa Do
Swing Thru and then boys you Run right
Ferris Wheel and do the Right and Left Thru
You'll Square Thru, three-quarters round the ringo
Swing that corner, Promenade
Oh Lord, it's hard to be humble
But I'm doing the best that I can

> *Sequence:*   Open, Figure twice Heads, Break, Figure twice
> Sides, Close

Suggested Singing Call Drill:

"God Bless America," Gold Star #GS 712, Caller — Cal Golden; original recording performed by Kate Smith.

Intro:

Four ladies Promenade go once around the ring
Get back home and Swing your man
Join hands; Circle to the Left; go round the ring
Left Allemande the corner; Weave the Ring
From the mountains to the prairies
Do sa do, Promenade
God Bless America, my home sweet home

Figure:

Head (side) couples Promenade go 1/2 way around
Down the middle and do the Right and Left Thru
Flutter Wheel across, Sweep and Quarter more
Pass Thru do a Right and Left Thru
Veer to the Left, Ferris Wheel
Center two Pass Thru
Swing the Corner Lady, Promenade
God Bless America, my home sweet home
My home sweet home, sides face Grand Square

Sequence: Intro, Figure twice Heads, Break, Figure twice sides, close

APPENDIX B

Record Sources

General Record Services for Square Dance Records (accept individual orders):

Merrback Record Service (Blue Star Record Company)
P.O. Box 7309
323 West 14th Street
Houston, Texas 77248-7309
(713) 862-7077

Palimino Square Dance Service
4440 Highway 63-S
Rochester, Minnesota 55904
(507) 282-4178
or
1-800-328-3800

Traditional Records:

The Lloyd Shaw Foundation Archives
1620 Los Alamos, SW
Albuquerque, New Mexico 87104
(505) 247-3921

Record Companies
(sell to dealers only)

Blue Star (See Merrbach Record Service.)

Chaparral
(formerly handled RoadRunners)
1425 Oakhill Drive
Plano, Texas 75075
(214) 423-7389

Gold Star Records Productions
P.O. Box 2274
Hot Springs, Arizona 71901
(501) 624-7274

Kalox
(Belco/Longhorn Records, Inc.)
2832 Live Oak Drive
Mesquite, Texas 75150
(214) 270-0616

Rhythm Records
2542 Palo Pinto
Houston, Texas 77080
(713) 462-1120

Rockin' A Records (See Merrbach Record Service.)

Sets In Order
(If record is unavailable, contact
Merrbach Record Service — E-Z School Rhythms)
462 North Robertson Boulevard
Los Angeles, California 90048
(216) 836-5591

Top
c/o Twel Grenn Enterprises, Inc.
P.O. Box 216
Bath, Ohio 44210
(216) 836-5591

(216) 836-5591

Windsor Records
312 Monterey Pass Road
Monterey Park, California 91754
(213) 282-5181

Traditional Square Dance Records:
The Lloyd Shaw Foundation
Recordings Division
Box 134
Sharpes, Florida 32959

Alcazar
Box 429
Waterbury, Vermont 05676

(Note: Contact the author concerning the availability of an instructional videocassette — 1/2 inch, VHS — to accompany this book. Send inquiries to: Professor Myrna M. Schild, Box 1126 — Dance, Southern Illinois University at Edwardsville, Edwardsville, Illinois, 62026-1126)

APPENDIX C

Bibliography

Books

Casey, Betty. *The Complete Book of Square (and Round Dancing)*. Garden City, NY: Double & Co., Inc., 1976.

Chase, Ann Hastings. *The Singing Caller*. New York: Association Press, 1947.

Harris, Pittman, Waller. *Dance Awhile*, 5th ed. Minneapolis, MN: Burgess Publishing.

Osgood, Bob. *The Caller/Teacher Manual*. Los Angeles, CA: SIOASDS, 1985.

Osgood, Bob. *The Callertext*. Los Angeles, CA : SIOASDS, 1985.

Phillips, Patricia A. *Contemporary Square Dance*. Dubuque, IA: William C. Brown Co., 1968.

Pamphlets & Magazines

Sets In Order American Square Dance Society, 462 North Robertson Blvd., Los Angeles, CA 90048

The Illustrated Basic Movements of Square Dancing. (Handbook Series — revised).

The Square Dance Indoctrination Handbook (revised).

The Square Dancing Magazine (1948 — 1985).

American Square Dance Magazine, P.O. Box 488, Huron, OH 44839

Square Dance Book Service
Diplomas: Square, Round, Clogging
Promotional folders

APPENDIX D

Clogging Terminology

Basic Movements
(Referred to as "Parts" of Basic Steps)

Brush (BR) A kicking motion in which only the toe tap sounds as it brushes the floor. The foot strikes the floor a glancing blow and continues moving in the direction of the kick (i.e., Brush Forward, Brush Back, Brush Across, Brush Back Across)

Double-Toe (DT) A short Brush Forward with an immediate Brush Back in a snapping motion, sounding only the toe tap, twice, bending knee upward after second tap, in the space of one beat.

Drag (DR) The second half of the Shuffle described below, usually done on one foot. With your weight on the foot and your knee slightly bent, straighten the knee and drag foot backward about half the length of your foot. Generally you slide on the entire foot, but movement may be done on toe tap only with a heel snap downward at the end of the slide.

Heel Implies that your weight is on the ball of your foot and is already resting on the floor—snap the heel down, sounding only the heel tap, shifting your weight onto the entire floor.

Hop (HP) All weight is on one foot; the other foot is off the floor. Hop just enough to clear the floor with the foot bearing your weight; land on that same foot with the heel and toe hitting at the same time.

Rock (RK) Step your weight onto the ball of your foot (preferably at the arch or even with the heel of the other foot), sounding the toe tap only, lifting the other foot off the floor during the same motion.

Slide (SL)   Done just as the first half of the shuffle, usually done on one foot. It is the last beat of your second basic step. Place weight on the toe with heel just slightly off the floor. Slide forward on the ball of your foot and snap down on your heel. It will probably feel to you that you are sliding the entire foot all at once.

Shuffle   With both feet flat on the floor, bend your knees and slide forward on your toe taps with the forward momentum of bending motion a distance about half the length of your foot, snapping the heels down to sound the heel taps; immediately straighten your knees and let the momentum drag your feet back to the starting position. (Shuffle is also done on only one foot, in the same way, while doing a Brush, Double-Toe, Slide, etc., on the other foot at the same time.) Same motion including movement of the feet, as Bend (Forward), Straighten (Back), Bend (Forward), Straighten (Back).

Step (ST)   Place total weight on the foot or shift weight from one foot to the other. Weight can be placed on just the toe or the entire foot. When placed on the entire foot, sound toe and heel taps at the same time.

Toe   Place weight on the ball of the foot with *definite* tap sound (beat/count/tap expression means the same — one sound, beat, or tap with the toe tap making the noise) while the heel remains off the floor; only the toe tap sounds.

Clogging Terminology and Basics as used by the Clogging/Hoedown Council, Walhalla, South Carolina. Taught by Bill Nichols, President of the Council.

Contact: Bill Nichols — Route 3, Box 307B, Walhalla, South Carolina, 29691, Don R. Allen — University of Northern Iowa, Cedar Falls, Iowa 50614, Violet Marsh — Houston, Texas, Sheila Popwell — Atlanta, Georgia, Terry Severns — St. Louis, Missouri (Ozark Cloggers-Happy Tappers).

CLOG STEP PATTERNS
(developed by Don R. Allen)

Shuffle (Both feet on floor)

&	1
DR -	SL

Shuffle with Lift (One foot on floor, the other off floor)

Double Toe Slide

&ah	1	&ah	2
DT-	SL-	DT-	SL
R	L	R	L

Double Toe Step

&ah	1	&ah	2
DT-	ST-	DT-	ST
R	R	L	L

Rock Step (in place)

&ah	1	&	2	&	3	&	4
DT-	ST-	RK-	ST-	RK-	ST-	RK-	ST
R	R	L	R	L	R	L	R

Variations:　　　1 - Turning to R or L
　　　　　　　　　2 - Moving side R or L
　　　　　　　　　3 - RK foot XIF (cross in front)

Single Basic

&ah	1	&	2
DT-	ST-	RK-	ST
R	R	L	R

Double Basic

&ah	1	&ah	2	&	3
DT-	ST-	DT-	ST-	RK-	ST
R	RS	L	L	R	L

Slide (SL)   Done just as the first half of the shuffle, usually done on one foot. It is the last beat of your second basic step. Place weight on the toe with heel just slightly off the floor. Slide forward on the ball of your foot and snap down on your heel. It will probably feel to you that you are sliding the entire foot all at once.

Shuffle   With both feet flat on the floor, bend your knees and slide forward on your toe taps with the forward momentum of bending motion a distance about half the length of your foot, snapping the heels down to sound the heel taps; immediately straighten your knees and let the momentum drag your feet back to the starting position. (Shuffle is also done on only one foot, in the same way, while doing a Brush, Double-Toe, Slide, etc., on the other foot at the same time.) Same motion including movement of the feet, as Bend (Forward), Straighten (Back), Bend (Forward), Straighten (Back).

Step (ST)   Place total weight on the foot or shift weight from one foot to the other. Weight can be placed on just the toe or the entire foot. When placed on the entire foot, sound toe and heel taps at the same time.

Toe   Place weight on the ball of the foot with *definite* tap sound (beat/count/tap expression means the same — one sound, beat, or tap with the toe tap making the noise) while the heel remains off the floor; only the toe tap sounds.

Clogging Terminology and Basics as used by the Clogging/Hoedown Council, Walhalla, South Carolina. Taught by Bill Nichols, President of the Council.

Contact: Bill Nichols — Route 3, Box 307B, Walhalla, South Carolina, 29691, Don R. Allen — University of Northern Iowa, Cedar Falls, Iowa 50614, Violet Marsh — Houston, Texas, Sheila Popwell — Atlanta, Georgia, Terry Severns — St. Louis, Missouri (Ozark Cloggers-Happy Tappers).

APPENDIX E

Basic Movements Checklist

For the person learning to square dance: Use this list to check these basics as they are taught. You may wish to put an X in front of the basic the first time the movement is taught and then later run a line through it when you have thoroughly learned the basic.

_____ 1. Circle Family
___ a. Circle Left
___ b. Circle Right
_____ 2. Forward and Back
_____ 3. Do Sa Do
_____ 4. Swing
_____ 5. Promenade Family
___ a. Couples (full, 1/2, 3/4)
___ b. Single File
___ c. Wrong Way
_____ 6. Allemande Family
___ a. Allemande Left
___ b. Left Arm Turn
___ c. Right Arm Turn
_____ 7. Right and Left Grand Family
___ a. Right and Left Grand
___ b. Weave the Ring
___ c. Wrong Way Grand
_____ 8. Star Family
___ a. Star by the Right
___ b. Star by the Left
_____ 9. Star Promenade
_____ 10. Pass Thru
_____ 11. Split Family
___ a. Split the Outside Couple
___ b. Split the Ring (one couple)
_____ 12. Half Sashay Family
___ a. Half Sashay
___ b. Rollaway
___ c. Ladies in, Men Sashay

_____ 13. Turn Back Family
___ a. U Turn Back
___ b. Gents or Ladies Backtrack
_____ 14. Separate Family
___ a. Separate
___ b. Divide
_____ 15. Courtesy Turn
_____ 16. Ladies Chain Family
___ a. Two Ladies (regular and 3/4)
___ b. Four Ladies (regular and 3/4)
_____ 17. Do Paso
_____ 18. Lead Right
_____ 19. Right and Left Thru
_____ 20. Grand Square
_____ 21. Star Thru
_____ 22. Circle to a Line
_____ 23. Bend the Line
_____ 24. All Around the Left Hand Lady
_____ 25. See Saw
_____ 26. Square Thru Family (1-5 hands)
___ a. Square Thru
___ b. Left Square Thru
_____ 27. California Twirl

_____ 28. **Dive Thru**
_____ 29. **Cross Trail Thru**
_____ 30. **Wheel Around**
_____ 31. **Thar Family**
___ a. Allemande Thar
___ b. *Wrong Way*
        Thar
_____ 32. **Shoot the Star**
        (Regular, full around)
_____ 33. **Slip the Clutch**
_____ 34. **Box the Gnat**
_____ 35. **Ocean Wave**
        Family
___ a. Right Hand Wave
___ b. *Left Hand Wave*
___ c. Alamo Style Wave
___ d. Wave Balance
_____ 36. **Pass the Ocean**
_____ 37. **Swing Thru Family**
___ a. Swing Thru — Right
___ b. Alamo Swing
        Thru
___ c. *Left Swing Thru*
_____ 38. **Run Family**
___ a. Boys Run
___ b. Girls Run
___ c. Ends Run
___ d. Centers Run
___ e. *Cross Run*
_____ 39. **Trade Family**
___ a. Boys Trade
___ b. Girls Trade
___ c. Ends Trade
___ d. Centers Trade
___ e. Couples Trade
___ f. Partners Trade

_____ 40. **Wheel and Deal**
        Family
___ a. From a Line of Four
___ b. From a
        Two-Faced Line
_____ 41. **Double Pass Thru**
_____ 42. **Zoom**
_____ 43. **Flutterwheel Family**
___ a. Flutterwheel
___ b. *Reverse*
        Flutterwheel
_____ 44. **Sweep 1/4**
_____ 45. **Veer Family**
___ a. Veer Left
___ b. Veer Right
_____ 46. **Trade By**
_____ 47. **Touch 1/4**
_____ 48. **Circulate Family**
___ a. Boys Circulate
___ b. Girls Circulate
___ c. All Eight Circulate
___ d. Ends Circulate
___ e. Centers Circulate
___ f. Couples Circulate
___ g. *Box Circulate*
___ h. *Single File*
        Circulate (column)
___ i. *Split Circulate*
_____ 49. **Ferris Wheel**

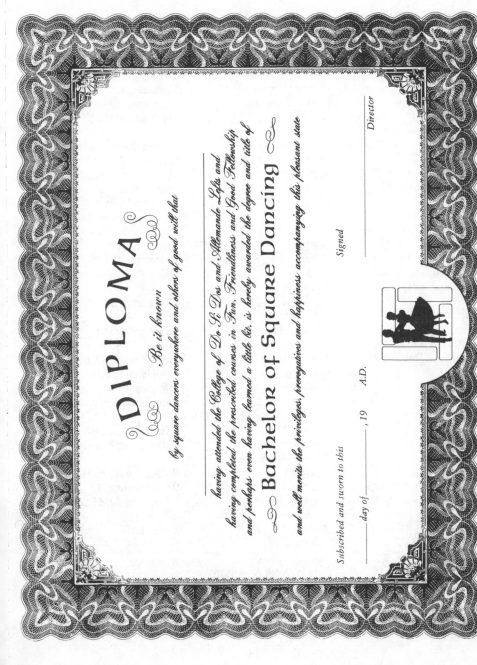

DIPLOMA

Be it known

by square dancers everywhere and others of good will that

_____

having attended the College of Do Si Dos and Allemande Lefts and
having completed the prescribed courses in Fun, Friendliness and Good Fellowship
and perhaps even having learned a little bit, is hereby awarded the degree and title of

Bachelor of Square Dancing

and well merits the privileges, prerogatives and happiness accompanying this pleasant state

Subscribed and sworn to this

_____ day of _____ , 19 ___ A.D.

Signed _____

_____
Director

INDEX

(References to illustrations are in boldface print.)